ONE PLUS ONE EQUALS THREE

Dave Trott is the author of *Creative Mischief* and *Predatory Thinking* and founded four award-winning ad agencies. Born in east London, he went to art school in New York on a Rockefeller Scholarship. From there he began an illustrious career in advertising, as part of the creative team behind 'Hello Tosh Gotta Toshiba', 'Aristonandonandon', the Cadbury Flake ads and many, many more. Dave's agency – Gold Greenlees Trott – was voted Agency of the Year by *Campaign* magazine, and Most Creative Agency in the World by *Ad Age* in New York. In 2004 he was given the D&AD President's Award for lifetime achievement in advertising.

By the same author:

CREATIVE MISCHIEF

PREDATORY THINKING

DAVE TROTT

ONE PLUS ONE EQUALS THREE

A MASTERCLASS IN CREATIVE THINKING

PAN BOOKS

First published 2015 by Macmillan

This paperback edition published 2016 by Pan Books
an imprint of Pan Macmillan
20 New Wharf Road, London N1 9RR
Associated companies throughout the world
www.panmacmillan.com

ISBN 978-1-4472-8705-6

9 8 7 6 5 4 3

A CIP catalogue record for this book is available from the British Library.

Printed and bound by CPI Group (UK) Ltd, Croydon, CR0 4YY

Visit **www.panmacmillan.com** to read more about all our books
and to buy them. You will also find features, author interviews and
news of any author events, and you can sign up for e-newsletters
so that you're always first to hear about our new releases.

CONTENTS

ONE PLUS ONE EQUALS THREE

INTRODUCTION:
WHY ONE PLUS ONE EQUALS THREE

A few years ago I read an interview with Steve Jobs.

Steve said any new idea is nothing more than a new combination of old elements.

He said the ability to make those new combinations depends on our ability to see relationships.

That's what makes some people more creative.

They are better at spotting those connections, better at recognizing possible relationships.

They are able to do this because they've had more experiences, or thought more about those experiences, than other people.

They are better at connecting the dots because they have more dots to connect.

Steve said that this was the problem in the 'creative' industries.

Most people haven't had diverse experiences.

They may know a lot, but only about a very narrow field.

So they don't have enough dots to connect.

And so they end up with predictable, linear solutions.

One of the best advertising people ever was Carl Ally.
He said the true creative person wants to be a know-it-all.
They want to know about all kinds of things: ancient history,
nineteenth-century mathematics, modern manufacturing
techniques, flower arranging, and lean hog futures.
Because they never know when these ideas might come
together to form a new idea.
It may happen six minutes later or six years down the road,
but they know it will happen.

That's been part of my purpose in this book.
The more varied the input, the more unexpected the
combinations, the more creative the ideas.
As Steve Jobs said: the broader our understanding of human
experience, the more dots we will have to connect, the more
creative our ideas will be.

Similarly, years ago I read a book by an Indian mathematics
professor.
She wrote that it's possible to greatly increase the amount of
brain we use.
But not in the conventional way.

In fact, in exactly the opposite way.

The secret again is connections.

Conventionally, people just learn more stuff.

They learn more stuff about whatever they're interested in.

She said this kind of learning made for small, slow growth in brain usage.

Because we are simply adding to the store of what we already know.

But if new ideas are new combinations of existing ideas, the more connections we can create, the more ideas we can generate.

That's why the professor said, for real growth, we need to identify the areas we're not naturally interested in.

Then we need to investigate those areas.

This massively multiplies the amount of new connections we can make with our existing store of knowledge.

Because it's no longer predictable, now it's original and surprising.

Because each connection will be a new connection with everything else we know.

So our creativity is directly related to how many connections we are able to make.

Which is directly related to how much new and unusual stuff we expose our minds to.

Which is the point of this book.

Under the old system 1 + 1 = 2

Under the new system 1 + 1 = 3

PART ONE

REGRET IS WORSE THAN EMBARRASSMENT

WHAT EXISTS BEATS WHAT DOESN'T

In 1988, Nicholas Winton's wife was going through their attic.

She came across a scrapbook.

In it were hundreds and hundreds of names and addresses.

She'd never seen them before.

She asked her husband what they were.

Then he told her this story.

In 1938, Nicholas Winton was going skiing in Switzerland.

When Kristallnacht happened.

In a night of violence, mass attacks were organized against Jews all over Germany.

Jewish homes, hospitals and schools were looted and burned.

Over 1,000 synagogues and 7,000 businesses were destroyed.

Nearly 100 people were murdered and 30,000 were arrested and sent to concentration camps.

It was the start of the Nazis' campaign to systematically destroy the Jewish race.

Nicholas Winton had friends in Prague.

He cancelled his skiing trip and went there instead.

It was obvious Germany would invade Czechoslovakia next and every Jewish person there would be exterminated.

Families were desperate to save their children.

The British government had agreed to allow unrestricted immigration of refugee Jewish children.

All they needed was fifty pounds each and a place to stay.

Nicholas Winton decided to take action.

He set up an office in the dining room of his hotel in Prague.

Made lists of hundreds of children he would help escape the Nazis.

Then he travelled back to Britain to arrange the money and the homes.

He arranged for 669 children to escape to Britain.

Children who wouldn't otherwise have survived.

We know this because, after the children left, their parents perished in the concentration camps.

Nicholas Winton never mentioned it to anyone because he felt frustrated that he hadn't done more.

Later, in 1988, he was in the audience at the recording of a TV programme.

Suddenly the host began talking about Nicholas Winton.

She introduced the lady next to him.

The lady, now in her fifties, was one of the children he had saved.

The lady said thank you, over and over again.

She kissed his hand and held it to her cheek.

And he had to wipe his eye as the good he had done became real to him in human terms.

Then the host asked if there was anyone else in the audience who owed their life to Nicholas Winton.

And the entire audience stood up.

People who had families of their own: wives, husbands, children, grandchildren.

And Nicholas Winton didn't quite know what was happening.

First he looked to one side, then the other, and then behind him.

Then he stood up and looked all around him.

And he couldn't believe it.

The entire audience, every single person in the TV studio, was standing up, smiling and thanking him.

Physicists, surgeons, authors, artists, politicians, journalists, architects, filmmakers, lawyers, businessmen, teachers.

He'd saved the life of every single person in the theatre.

And Nicholas Winton finally got it.

Forget what you haven't done.

It's what you have done that matters.

WHAT *AREN'T* THEY DOING?

David Geffen was Jewish. He was born in Brooklyn.

But he wanted to go live among the 'beautiful people', so when he was 18 he moved to LA.

The trouble was, he wasn't any good at anything, and he got fired from every single job.

He was talking to a struggling actor about this.

The actor said, 'You can't do anything? You should be an agent, they don't do anything.'

Geffen took him seriously; he got a job at the William Morris Agency.

He got a job in the mailroom, and he had to lie to get it.

On his CV he said he had a degree from UCLA.

He figured it didn't matter, no one would check.

Then he found out the guy working next to him had just been fired for claiming he'd graduated from CCNY on his CV.

So they did check.

Luckily Geffen was in the mailroom, so he got in early every morning and went through the mail.

A few weeks later he intercepted the letter from UCLA.

He steamed it open and changed one word.

He changed 'David Geffen *never* graduated from UCLA' to 'David Geffen *recently* graduated from UCLA.'

Plus his boss thought he was a good example, starting work early every day, so he raised Geffen's salary.

While Geffen was delivering the office mail he watched what the agents did.

He thought, 'All they do is bullshit on the phone all day. I can do that. I can bullshit on the phone.'

It's a well-known fact that guys from Brooklyn are better at bullshitting than anyone else.

And he noticed what they were doing was trying to sign established acts.

This made no sense.

Established acts were more expensive, and competition to sign them was greater.

To Geffen it made sense to find the acts before they were established.

So that's what he did.

While all the other agents were at home with their families, Geffen would go to clubs and bars and find talent before anyone else.

He'd sign people who didn't already have agents.

And he became the most successful agent at William Morris.

He was so good that he opened his own record label by the time he was 27: Asylum Records.

The artists he made famous on this label included Neil Young, Crosby, Stills and Nash, the Eagles, Joni Mitchell, Jackson Browne, Tom Waits, Elton John, Judee Sill.

Asylum produced some of the best, and bestselling, records of the 1970s.

In 1972 he sold the company, and eventually he left.

Five years later he opened Geffen Records.

This time he signed artists like Donna Summer, Cher, Aerosmith, Guns N' Roses, Nirvana, The Stone Roses.

But he really wanted to sign John Lennon.

The problem was so did everyone else.

Geffen thought, 'How do I get upstream of this problem?'

So he did what no one else was doing.

The other labels were talking directly to John Lennon.

Geffen figured that Yoko Ono must feel excluded.

So he didn't talk to Lennon, he talked to Yoko Ono.

Geffen persuaded her, and then she persuaded Lennon.

He signed to Geffen's label and released the *Double Fantasy* album, his masterpiece.

Geffen Records was a massive success.

In 1990, Geffen sold it and a few years later he left.

He left to open a movie studio with Steven Spielberg: Dreamworks SKG (Geffen is the G).

Geffen is now worth around $6 billion.

Not by being better, or tougher, or faster, or smarter, or richer, or better educated than other people.

Not by trying to beat other people at their own game.

But by looking at other people and thinking, 'What *aren't* they doing?'

NOTHING TO FEAR BUT FEAR ITSELF

My dad left school at 13, most people did in those days.

He started work on a building site.

Houses in east London didn't have interior plumbing then.

So at 6 a.m. every day, he got up, went into the back yard and broke the ice off the tap.

Then he'd take his shirt off and have a wash.

In the evenings, after work, when everyone else went to the pub, he didn't go with them.

He went home and taught himself to read and write properly, so that he could get a better job.

And he passed the exam to join the police.

That was pretty much the pattern of Dad's life.

Whatever he didn't like, whatever made him uncomfortable, he didn't run away from it.

He faced it head-on and out-thought it.

When he was a young copper, he worked in south London.

He was put on the night shift.

The streets still had gas lights then, so you had eight hours out in the poorly lit streets, totally alone.

Your mind would play tricks on you.

Dad decided the best way to beat the fear was to face it.

So about 2 a.m. he headed towards the middle of Tooting Bec Common.

Tooting Bec Common was a very large area of wild land.

There was nothing there except some woods with a lunatic asylum and a graveyard in the middle.

That's where he went.

Obviously everything was pitch black, no street lights, no light at all.

The only sound was the snapping of twigs under his boots.

And the piercing screams from the asylum.

Dad would head towards the graveyard.

Then he'd feel around for one of the crooked, overgrown graves.

Then he'd sit on it, unwrap his sandwich and make himself slowly eat it.

Training himself not to be afraid of the dark.

Not to believe whatever horrors his mind made up.

He said the worst time was when he was walking through the woods and he felt something brush against his face.

He reached out to see what it was.

It was a foot, which as he carefully felt upwards was attached to a slowly swinging leg.

In the pitch black, Dad had to get the body down.

Then slowly feel it all over, in the dark, to check it wasn't breathing.

Meanwhile, the only sounds were the screams from the lunatic asylum.

And what he hoped were animals walking around the graves.

Dad later found out one of the lunatics had escaped from the asylum and hanged himself.

It wasn't pleasant, but that was how he out-thought his fear of the dark.

He put himself in a place that was worse than his imagination, and he beat it.

He beat his own imagination.

Which is where reality starts.

Dad never knew anything about Buddha.

But I think he would have understood what Buddha had said over 2,000 years earlier:

'Nothing can harm a man so much as his own thoughts untamed.'

NOT-SO-SMART BOMB

Hollywood often makes films about nuclear bombs.

How someone got hold of one and is threatening a city.

These films aren't usually very scary because we all know they're not real.

Except one day in 1983, it nearly happened.

And it was much, much worse than the Hollywood version.

Because it wasn't just a single nuclear bomb.

It was hundreds and hundreds of nuclear bombs.

By this time, the USA and USSR had been ready to release every single one of their nuclear weapons at each other for thirty years.

Each side was convinced the other side was about to do it.

The only question was who would be first.

It's estimated that the two countries had enough nuclear weapons to destroy the world 20 times over.

All just sitting in bunkers, warmed up, ready to go.

By 1983, the Soviets had built a brand new early warning system called Oko.

Ready to detect the very first launch of an American missile attack.

A state-of-the-art system, it did away with the possibility of human error.

On 26 September 1983, Stanislav Petrov was in charge of Oko.

He was a lieutenant colonel in the Soviet Strategic Air Defence Forces.

At half past midnight, a warning light came on and a siren started screaming.

Oko showed a missile being launched from the USA.

Everyone in the control room froze.

Then a second warning light and siren showed another missile.

Then a third missile.

Then a fourth missile.

Then a fifth.

This was an all-out nuclear attack on the USSR.

Petrov had clear orders.

Pick up the phone and order a nuclear response.

If he waited too long, the American missiles would hit and destroy all the Soviet missile bases.

Their country would be utterly destroyed.

Millions upon millions dead, and those left alive at the mercy of the Americans.

His orders were clear.

But Stanislav Petrov didn't follow the orders.

He sat and thought for a minute.

And he did the unthinkable.

He questioned the foolproof computer system.

And he allowed human reasoning to override the computer.

He thought, Why only five missiles if it's an all-out attack?

And he decided the computer was wrong.

He refused to pick up the phone and report an attack.

As the seconds crawled by, his uniform became drenched in sweat.

Everyone in the control room watched him and held their breath.

Until the truth was confirmed.

Ground radar and geostationary satellites reported there were no American missile launches.

The supposedly foolproof system had misread a one-in-a-million alignment of the sun's rays on high-altitude clouds.

There were no US missiles launched at the Soviet Union.

And, thanks to one man, no Soviet missiles launched at the US.

It was many years before the story finally emerged.

When it did, Stanislav Petrov was invited to the United Nations and given the World Citizen Award in 2006.

Is it an overreaction to say his decision saved the world?

Later, a Soviet General described what would have happened if the Soviets had launched their missiles.

'About half of France, half of Germany, 30% of the USA, and all of Britain would have been destroyed.'

In a lesson for all of us, Stanislav Petrov explained why he had halted the launch.

Something we could all bear in mind when dealing with technology today.

He said, 'The computer is by definition brainless. There are many things it can mistake for a missile launch.'

There you have it from the man who saved the world.

The computer isn't good, it isn't bad.

It's brainless.

As living, thinking humans, we have no excuse.

It's worth taking a moment to think.

Otherwise the results might be catastrophic.

REGRET IS WORSE THAN EMBARRASSMENT

Tilly Smith was 10 years old.

She was on holiday with her little sister Holly and her mum and dad.

They'd gone to a sunny place called Mai Khao Beach.

One day, they got up early and walked along the beach in the sun.

As they were walking, Tilly noticed the tide had gone out.

A very, very long way out.

She also noticed that the water was frothy, just like a pint of beer.

She stopped dead.

This was exactly like the newsreel film her geography teacher had shown her back at school in Surrey.

Mr Kearney had shown her class some old black and white footage of Hawaii in 1946.

It was the only film anyone had ever seen of a tsunami.

In fact, most people hadn't even heard the word tsunami.

But Tilly was convinced that was what was happening right now.

She tried to explain to her mum.

Her mum wasn't convinced, obviously.

No one had heard of a tsunami.

No one on the beach, including the lifeguards, was taking any notice.

So this probably happened all the time.

How could a 10-year-old girl from Surrey know more than the people who lived and worked here?

Tilly started to yell at her dad.

She was positive this was the thing Mr Kearney had shown them two weeks before.

Her dad had a difficult choice.

Listen to his 10-year-old daughter, who was getting hysterical, and cause panic on the beach.

Or ignore it and just take his daughter back to the hotel until she calmed down.

But what if she was right?

All these families, all these children, would die, and he'd be responsible.

For an Englishman, embarrassment is the worst thing of all.

But he decided he had to take a chance.

He told the security guards, who told the lifeguards.

The beach was cleared and everyone went back to the hotel and climbed to the third floor.

And waited.

They didn't have to wait long.

In less than a minute the first of three giant waves struck.

Those giant waves struck beaches all over South East Asia that morning.

It was the Boxing Day tsunami of 2004.

By the end of the day everyone in the world knew what a tsunami was.

Because that tsunami killed a quarter of a million people on beaches in thirteen different countries.

But there was one beach where no one died.

Mai Khao Beach, Thailand.

The beach Tilly Smith had been on.

That was the beach everyone left before the wave struck.

Because 10-year-old Tilly refused to shut up.

She wasn't old enough to be silenced by crushing embarrassment.

She was still young enough to know she was right, and wouldn't allow herself to be quietened down.

Later she was taken to the United Nations, where she was publicly congratulated by Bill Clinton.

Because Tilly saved the lives of over 100 people.

Men, women and children.

By being unreasonable.

By insisting on being heard.

Instead of wishing she'd spoken up after it was too late.

That's something we could all do with learning.

Regret is worse than embarrassment.

WHAT'S DUMB IS GIVING UP

John Lasseter always wanted to be an animator.

His dream, of course, was to work at Disney.

But his first job there was in the theme park, on the Jungle Cruise ride.

Eventually, he managed to get a job in the animation studio.

Then something really exciting happened.

He saw the beginnings of the film *Tron*, a live action movie enhanced by digital effects.

Lasseter saw the possibilities for animation.

Up until that time, all animation had been hand-drawn 2D.

His vision was an entirely computer-animated 3D movie.

But Disney studios had been making 2D movies for fifty years.

They didn't need to be told what to do by some dumb, argumentative kid.

So John Lasseter was fired.

Now he didn't have his dream job anymore.

He got a job at another digital company working on enhancements for George Lucas's films.

Lasseter was the only animator there, and he managed to make a very short, very interesting, computer-animated film.

Then he got lucky.

George Lucas sold his company to Steve Jobs.

Jobs paid $10 million, thinking he was just getting a computer hardware company.

But then John Lasseter showed him the short film he'd made.

Jobs asked him what he needed to make a success of his part of the company.

Lasseter said they needed to make a longer film, but that it would cost half a million dollars.

Jobs wrote out a personal cheque.

But before he handed it to Lasseter he said, 'Just one thing, John.'

Lasseter thought, here it comes, all the terms and conditions and stifling restrictions.

But Steve Jobs said, 'Just make it great.'

And handed over the cheque.

And John Lasseter did make it great, that film won an Oscar.

That film was *Toy Story*, the first feature film in history produced using computer animation.

And that film launched the new company, now called Pixar.

And Pixar went on to launch an entirely new style of animation.

Totally computer-generated 3D feature films.

Pixar made some of the most successful films of all time: *Toy Story*, *A Bug's Life*, *The Incredibles*, *Wall-E*, *Up*.

In fact, *Toy Story 3* became the first film ever to gross a billion dollars.

Up became the first animated film to open the Cannes Film Festival.

John Lasseter became the first animator ever, including Walt Disney, to win the David O. Selznick Award.

The Museum of Modern Art in New York even staged a '20 Years of Pixar' exhibition.

Meanwhile, Disney was in serious trouble.

Their old-fashioned animation style had been totally eclipsed by Pixar.

So in 2006, Disney made a deal to buy Pixar for $7.7 billion.

From his initial $10 million investment, Steve Jobs made a profit of $3.7 billion.

As a condition of the deal, Disney insisted John Lasseter must take over Disney animation.

The company he'd been fired from as a junior.

It was written into the contract.

And so he became Chief Creative Officer of Disney and Pixar.

John Lasseter now has his own star on Hollywood's Walk of Fame.

And two Disney rides, 'Finding Nemo' and 'A Bug's Land', are taken from his movies.

Similar rides to the one he used to work on when he started.

It seems the 'dumb kid' wasn't so dumb after all.

MIND BLOWING

In the nineteenth century, America wanted to unite the
continent by blasting tunnels through mountains of rock.

But there was a problem.

The most powerful explosive was nitroglycerine.

It came in liquid form and was incredibly unstable.

Any sudden shock could detonate it.

It was so powerful it could save hundreds of workers months
of backbreaking digging.

So it was used by gold-miners, oil-well drillers, rock
tunnellers.

But conditions were never ideal.

It might be steep, or dark, or wet.

And that meant someone might slip and drop the
nitroglycerine.

Which wasn't good news.

As well as the deaths in the mines and tunnels, there were
larger tragedies in nearby towns.

In 1866, a crate of nitroglycerine was shipped via Wells Fargo.

The crate was found to be leaking.

The clerks thought they'd better open it and check the
contents.

They tried to open the crate with a hammer and chisel.

The blast killed 15 people.

Windows were blown out half a mile away.

The local newspaper reported a human arm stuck on a third floor ledge and a human vertebra found on the next street.

In San Francisco, a nitroglycerine factory exploded.

15 people were killed and the blast was heard 40 miles away.

Locals thought it was an earthquake.

Papers reported human remains scattered along the road for a mile.

Back in 1864, even Alfred Nobel's younger brother had been killed in an explosion.

Alfred Nobel was a scientist and a pacifist.

He decided to make nitroglycerine safe.

He discovered he could mix it with a certain type of earth to create a paste.

The paste was stable and wouldn't explode until ignited.

He called his invention dynamite.

Dynamite could be made into sausage shapes that could be packed into holes for blasting.

It could be transported or dropped without exploding.

Dynamite saved a lot of lives, and it made Nobel a rich man.

As a pacifist, he felt he'd helped make the world a better place.

Until his older brother died of an illness.

A French newspaper confused the brothers and reported the death as if it was Alfred Nobel himself.

The headline said, 'NOBEL, THE MERCHANT OF DEATH, IS DEAD'.

He was shocked.

The paper went on to describe him as 'The man who got rich by finding ways to kill more people faster than ever before.'

He couldn't believe it.

In his reality he was a humanitarian for discovering dynamite.

In their reality he was a monster for discovering dynamite.

That wasn't how he wanted to be remembered.

Nobel decided *he* would dictate the way he'd be remembered, not the newspapers.

So he founded the Nobel Awards.

Each year, a prize is awarded for Science, Chemistry, Medicine, Literature, and a special 'Nobel Peace Prize'.

It is now seen as the ultimate prize, the one every scientist and statesman really wants to win.

The award that can define a career.

And the name Nobel is now remembered just the way he wanted.

For the most prestigious humanitarian prize in the world.

Not the way the newspapers wanted, as 'The Merchant of Death'.

PART TWO

CHOICE ARCHITECTURE

CHOICE ARCHITECTURE

At a school in the USA, the girls in their early teens had just discovered lipstick.

They would go into the female toilets to apply it.

Then, giggling, they'd leave imprints of their lips on the large mirror.

This made a lot of extra work for the cleaning staff.

The head teacher asked the girls to stop.

Of course, they ignored her.

So she took the girls to the toilets for a demonstration.

She said, 'It takes a lot of work to clean the lipstick off the mirror.'

She said to the janitor, 'Please show the girls how much work it takes.'

The janitor put the mop in the toilet, squeezed off the excess water and washed the mirror.

Then put the mop in the toilet again, and repeated the process.

From that day on there was no more lipstick on the mirror.

That's choice architecture.

Don't try to force or nag people into doing what you want.

Accept that they are free to choose.

But you help them choose what you want.

The girls could still choose to kiss the mirror.

But now they know that their lips are touching the water from the toilets that everyone uses.

Suddenly it's not such an attractive idea.

No one wants to be kissed by lips with water from public toilet on them.

The girls are still free to choose.

But the architecture of the choice encourages them in a certain direction.

Just as architecture encourages people to use buildings in a particular way.

You design the building the way you want people to use it.

That way you don't have to nag people.

The National Portrait Gallery's problem was that very few people visited the upper floors, while the ground floor was always packed.

People couldn't be bothered to climb flights of stairs.

So they borrowed an idea from Frank Lloyd Wright's Guggenheim building in New York.

They changed the entrance.

They installed a large escalator right by it, taking visitors straight up to the top floor.

The exhibition now started at the top floor, and worked its way down to the ground floor.

The stairs were now for walking down not up.

Quite literally, choice architecture.

A writer at our agency, Rob DeCleyn, found another great example of choice architecture in his local paper.

A village in Kent had a problem with litter.

Sweet wrappers, crisp packets, soft drink cans and bottles were strewn all over the streets.

But the local shopkeeper didn't complain or nag the children.

He just wrote their name on the crisp and sweet packets when they bought them.

That's all, just the child's name.

And the litter problem cleared up almost immediately.

That's choice architecture.

The children could still choose to throw their wrappers in the street.

They didn't *have* to put them in the litter bin.

The only difference was that now everyone would know whose litter it was.

See, you don't have to threaten, or restrict or dictate anyone's choices.

If you're clever, you can just rearrange the architecture.

READING SETS YOU FREE

The problem with all prisons worldwide is overcrowding.
New prisoners come in, but the old ones keep coming back
too.
And all their time inside is spent with other criminals.
That's their environment, that's their only world.
But how do you change that?
How do you rehabilitate them, when there's no incentive for
them to change?
How do you show them there is a world outside that isn't
just about crime?
A world with more possibilities.
How do you get them to *care*?
You need to find a way to incentivize them.
To make them want to learn.
In Brazil that's just what they are doing.
They have a programme called Redemption Through Reading.
When a prisoner finishes a book, they get four days off their
sentence.
Simple as that.
The books are from an approved list: literary, philosophical
and scientific.
They get a month to read it and have to write an essay
showing they understood it.

The essay needs to 'use legible joined-up writing, and be free of corrections'.

They can do this with up to twelve books a year.

Which means that in just one year a Brazilian prisoner can wipe up to 7 weeks off their sentence.

They can work off as much as a year from a seven-year sentence.

Up to two years off a fourteen-year sentence.

So there's a practical reason to read books: to get out of prison earlier.

But while prisoners are reading, they also learn that another way of life exists.

They learn the habit of reading books to acquire knowledge.

They learn there are other possibilities in the outside world.

São Paulo lawyer Andre Kehdi runs a book-donation project for prisons.

He said, 'This way a person can leave prison more enlightened and with an enlarged view of the world.

Without doubt they will leave a better person.'

But does it work?

Guardian columnist Erwin James thinks it does.

He was a convicted murderer, serving life in an English prison.

Reading books transformed him as a person, and he was released after serving 20 years of a life sentence.

In the *Guardian*, he writes, 'The books I read in prison didn't get me a reduction in time, but they helped me become the person I always should have been.'

The books which initially had the most impact on him were, perhaps not surprisingly, about prison: *Prisoners of Honour*, *Crime and Punishment*, *One Day in the Life of Ivan Denisovich*, *Borstal Boy*.

These were the books that helped him to see his own situation in a new light.

Books which helped him understand it and, more importantly, to turn it around.

These books led him into the wider world of literature.

Erwin James has now written two bestselling books of his own, and works for charities as well as writing a column for the *Guardian*.

All because he started reading books in prison.

The purpose of a prison shouldn't just be locking people away, that's inefficient.

It should be about changing behaviour.

IT BEGGARS BELIEF

I saw a great photo of an American beggar.

He was sitting on the pavement with nine bowls in front of him, labelled as follows:

Muslim, Atheist, Jewish, Hindu, Buddhist, Agnostic, Christian.

Next to them was a handwritten sign that read: 'Which religion cares the most about the homeless?'

This is a beggar who understands advertising and behavioural economics.

Instead of talking about what he wants, he concentrates on what his audience wants.

In advertising terms it goes like this.

Start with the brief:

What does he want and who does he want it from?

What he wants is charity.

So, what will generate charity?

Compassion generates charity.

So, who has compassion?

Religious people apparently have compassion.

So, he creates a spirit of competitive compassion.

Each person wants their religion to appear more compassionate.

You can prove your religion is more compassionate by voting.

And you vote with your money.

Over the course of the day, everyone can see who's winning and losing, who's the most compassionate and who's the least.

And you can affect the result by simply adding more money.

At the end of the day, the beggar takes the money.

Then, tomorrow, the voting starts again.

The bowls with most in were Atheist, Buddhist, and Agnostic.

As well as lots of coins, these bowls even had folding money in them.

In America at least, these are not religions that people are traditionally born into.

They are choices that people make for themselves.

Consequently, they are more likely to feel strongly about them.

So they are more likely to care what other people think.

The other bowls had less in them: Muslim, Christian, Hindu, Jewish.

These are more likely to be inherited religions.

People are born into them, so they are likely to feel less strongly and care less about what others think.

The people who chose their belief system – Agnostics, Atheists, Buddhists – felt more competitive about it.

The people who were less likely to have actively chosen their religion – Muslims, Christians, Jewish and Hindus – weren't so competitive.

By sorting out what he wanted and who he wanted it from, that beggar was able to work out a brief.

It doesn't have to be complicated:

What do I want?

Who do I want it from?

Why should they do it (what's in it for them)?

By knowing that, he already understands more about strategic advertising creativity than most of the people working in it.

SAY IT WITH FLOWERS

As I write, it's 7 February and I'm sitting at my laptop.

I got up this morning thinking, I must remember to send my wife some flowers for Valentine's Day.

Being a bloke, I forgot.

I meant to remember yesterday.

I meant to remember the day before that.

Being a bloke, it keeps going straight out of my mind.

Then five minutes ago, the phone rang.

It was one of the flower shops I'd been meaning to call.

One of the four I have listed in my Filofax.

A very pleasant young lady said, 'Good morning, Mister Trott, Wild At Heart here. I've just noticed that last year you sent your wife some flowers for Valentine's Day, and I just wondered if you wanted to do the same again this year.'

How brilliant is that?

Look at the simple facts.

Every year, Valentine's Day falls on exactly the same date, 14 February.

Every year, millions of men send flowers to wives and sweethearts.

Now what men have in common is that they do it because they have to, not because they want to.

It's a distress purchase.

That's why they have trouble remembering things like flowers.

But they know they'll be in terrible trouble with the Mrs if they forget.

This is a terrific predatory opportunity for a smart flower shop.

Instead of worrying about how many customers will phone up wanting flowers this year, pre-empt it.

Make the calls to a soft target, the men who called you last year.

You know men will leave it to the last minute.

You know that means you won't know exactly how many flowers to order.

So make the calls a week or so early.

Before the men have had time to forget about it, panic, and call up at the last minute.

That way you can get their orders before the men have a chance to call any other shop.

You'll know well in advance exactly how many flowers you'll need on the day.

You can stagger your orders from your suppliers rather than having to risk ordering too many and being left with more than you can sell.

Or, worse still, not ordering enough and having to turn away last-minute callers to your competitors.

This is an example of really smart predatory thinking.

Getting the jump on your competitors by making life easier for a massive group of customers.

Just by picking the low hanging fruit: men.

The people who you know want flowers and will be massively relieved that you've taken the problem off their hands.

You take all your competition out of the game by getting to the customers before they do.

Because you're active while they're passive.

You pick up the phone and dial while they're sitting waiting for it to ring.

And with that thoroughness and attention to detail I know they'll do a better job on the bouquet itself.

I'm reassured.

I can relax.

Meanwhile, I have three other flower shops sitting in my Filofax wondering whether I'm going to be ringing them up this year.

UNCONVENTIONAL WISDOM

When my son was small, his teacher said she wanted a word with us.

The problem was that Lee kept swinging on the bannister in the stairwell.

Three floors above concrete stairs.

They'd told him to stop, but he kept doing it.

She asked if I could talk to him and make him stop.

I knew just telling him to stop wasn't going to cut it.

Any more than anti-drink driving, fire prevention or anti-smoking ads won't stop road accidents, fires or lung cancer.

Those ads that tell you that the result of your behaviour will be bad.

Driving drunk and killing people is bad.

Setting fire to your house is bad.

Dying from smoking cigarettes is bad.

Yes, we understand that, but we don't think it will happen to us.

So, instead of just telling my son not to swing on the bannisters, I thought there must be a better way.

And I waited until Saturday when my wife went out shopping.

Then I said to him, 'I'm going to teach you the proper way to fall down stairs.'

He thought this sounded fun and naughty: two things little boys like.

I took him to the top of our stairs.

I said, 'Now, the most important thing is to protect your head. So put your arms up either side of your head like this. Now roll yourself into a ball. That way, when you fall you'll do less damage. Have a go.'

And he fell down the stairs.

He got up and said, 'Ouch, that hurt.'

I said, 'That's because you're not doing it right, look: arms up, roll into a ball. Now try again.'

He did it and fell down the stairs again.

He got up rubbing his arms and legs.

I said, 'You've nearly got it. Try it again, arms up tight around your head, body rolled up into a tight ball.'

And he fell down the stairs again.

This time, as he was getting up, my wife came back from shopping.

She said, 'What's going on?'

I explained I was teaching him how to fall down stairs.

She said, 'Are you mad?'

I took her aside and said, 'Look at it this way, the school wants us to stop him swinging on the bannister. If he falls he'll drop three floors onto concrete steps and could break his back. But he doesn't know that, he's too young.

He just thinks it will never happen.

If we wait for him to find out how much it hurts it could be too late. So I'm doing several things here.

I'm teaching him that it's painful, but I'm teaching him on a single-storey staircase with fitted padded carpet, so he can't do himself too much harm.

Also, if he does break anything, I'm here to get him straight to A&E.

And, also, if he remembers to put his arms up and roll into a ball, he'll protect his head.

So even if he does do it at school, it will minimize the damage.'

And my wife calmed down a bit.

She still wasn't happy about it, but she could see the sense in it.

My son went off rubbing his arms.

Now he knew it hurt.

Later, the school told us he'd stopped swinging on the bannister.

Don't just go with conventional wisdom.

Don't keep repeating the same old solution even though we know it doesn't work.

Get upstream and change the problem.

Find a new solution, one that does work.

FRAMING AND REFRAMING

As a religion, Jainism is older than Christianity.

But, in my opinion, it's considerably more enlightened.

One of the main teachings of Jainism is that all truth is relative.

The limitations of human beings mean that no one can ever know the whole truth about anything.

Just the truth from their perspective.

This is illustrated by the parable of five blind men walking into an elephant.

Each tries to describe what they've bumped into.

One blind man feels the side of the elephant.

He says, 'An elephant is like a wall.'

Another blind man feels the elephant's trunk.

He says, 'No, an elephant is like a snake.'

The third blind man feels the leg.

He says, 'You're both wrong, an elephant is like a tree.'

The fourth blind man feels the tusk.

He says, 'Sorry, but an elephant is like a spear.'

The fifth blind man feels the tail.

He says 'You're all wrong, an elephant is like a piece of rope.'

All of the blind men mistake their little bit of truth for the whole truth.

This is what we all do, we can't help it.

Nobel prize-winning psychologist Daniel Kahneman calls this 'framing'.

He demonstrates that we can reverse someone's preference by presenting the same facts in different ways.

In an experiment, he asked participants to imagine an outbreak of disease that was expected to kill 600 people.

He gave them a choice:

Option A: 200 people will definitely be saved.

Option B: 1/3 probability all will be saved, 2/3 probability no one will be saved.

When asked, 75% of people chose option A.

He presented the same choice differently to the second group:

Option C: 400 people will definitely die.

Option D: 1/3 probability no one will die, 2/3 probability everyone will die.

This time the preference was reversed, 75% of people chose option D.

Even though options A and C are the same, and options B and D are the same.

By 'reframing' identical facts he made the choices appear totally different.

Digital entrepreneur and author Seth Godin calls this the 'compared to what?' syndrome.

Is the glass half-empty or half-full?

The answer is always 'compared to what?'

The glass is half-empty if the person next to us has a full glass.

The glass is half-full if the person next to us has an empty glass.

We live our lives in a constant state of comparison.

So constant that we don't even notice it.

And that should be the main purpose of all planning and research.

Context.

What is the context we are speaking into?

What is the context we want to create?

Control the context and you control the choice.

WHEN THE PEN IS MIGHTIER THAN THE SWORD

To consolidate their hold on the Holy Lands, the Crusaders built a series of massive castles.

The strongest of these was Krak des Chevaliers in Tripoli.

It was manned by the Knights Hospitaller.

Two thousand of the finest, toughest soldiers in the world.

The castle took a hundred years to build.

It controlled the entire region.

Even the mighty Saladin, at the peak of his power, couldn't capture it.

Krak des Chevaliers was seen as 'the key to the Christian lands'.

In 1260, Sultan Baibars came to power.

Babairs united what is now Syria and Egypt, and in 1271 he marched on Krak des Chevaliers.

He laid siege to the castle and eventually breached the outer wall.

His troops poured through, thinking the job was done.

Only to be confronted by the real castle.

The main part of Krak des Chevaliers had been built inside the outer walls.

First there was the moat.

So deep, it was useless to try tunnelling under it.

So wide, siege engines couldn't possibly cross it.

Then the castle walls, so thick they were impossible to penetrate.

And sloped, so no siege towers could be placed against them.

While Sultan Baibars contemplated the castle, the defenders simply killed off the attackers.

Now the Knights Hospitaller simply had to wait until reinforcements arrived.

They had already sent a secret message to the Grand Master of the Knights Hospitaller in Tripoli.

So they waited.

Conditions grew grim, but at least the invaders had no hope of penetrating the Krak des Chevaliers.

Eventually a reply was smuggled into the castle.

The Grand Master had no reinforcements to send, no one would be coming to relieve them.

However, the Grand Master understood the gravity of their situation and gave them permission to negotiate terms for surrender.

So that's what the Knights Hospitaller did.

They left the castle in return for safe passage for everyone inside.

They abandoned Krak des Chevaliers to Sultan Baibars and his troops.

'The key to the Christian lands' fell.

And with their power base gone, the Crusaders were driven from the Middle East.

The fall of the impregnable Krak des Chevaliers had been a massive shock to everyone.

Not least to the Grand Master of the Knights Hospitaller in Tripoli.

Because, and this is the part of the whole story I love best, he never got a letter asking for reinforcements.

It was intercepted by Sultan Baibar's troops.

And Baibar himself wrote the reply giving the Knights permission to surrender.

Which saved months of useless fighting and thousands of lives.

And lead to the conquest of the entire Christian forces.

How's that for changing a problem you can't solve into one you can?

PART THREE

THE SPIRIT OF THE LAW, NOT THE LETTER OF THE LAW

FALSE ECONOMICS

Between 1750 and 1810, London doubled in size from 750,000 to 1.5 million people.

It was the largest, most overcrowded city in the world.

It hadn't grown by plan, it just happened.

Consequently, the infrastructure wasn't set up for that many people.

People just dossed down wherever they could.

There were no sewers in those days, every house had a cesspit.

That meant 200,000 cesspits all over London.

And most of them were overflowing.

Into the alleys, into the streets, then back into the houses.

Down the walls and into the basements where the poorest slept.

A quick fix was to divert all that raw sewage into the drains.

The drains that carried the rainwater into the Thames.

The Thames, where the water companies pumped the drinking water from.

And two massive cholera outbreaks killed tens of thousands of people.

But it wasn't until the 'Big Stink' of 1858 that the authorities took much notice.

The Thames flows right past Parliament, and the stench of raw sewage was so overpowering that the enormous hanging curtains in the House of Commons had to be soaked in chloride of lime.

But even that couldn't cover the 'Big Stink'.

So Joseph Bazalgette, Chief Engineer of the Metropolitan Board of Works, designed and built the first system of enclosed sewers.

A massive, entirely brick-built project.

Over a thousand miles of street sewers, which would empty into eighty miles of main sewers, all of it underground.

And take all that human waste away from London.

But the part that impresses me most was the way Bazalgette designed the sewers.

He took into account everyone living in London.

He made the diameter of the sewers more than enough to handle everyone's waste.

Then he did something unthinkable to most people.

He doubled it.

Let's repeat that.

He calculated the most that could possibly be needed.

Then he *doubled* it.

Bazalgette said, 'We're only going to be doing this once. We'd better allow for the unforeseen.'

If only everyone had that much nous.

To allow for the unforeseen.

What no one could possibly have foreseen when Bazalgette built those sewers was what would happen a hundred years in the future.

In the 1960s, councils all over London would be building massive high-rise blocks of flats.

Huge multi-storey dwellings everywhere, emptying their waste into those hundred-year-old Victorian sewers.

If Bazalgette had stuck to the original specification, the sewers would have overflowed back up into the streets.

But they didn't.

Because Bazalgette didn't try to get away with the bare minimum.

The way most people do.

Spend absolutely the least possible amount we can get away with.

Do the job on as tight a budget as possible.

Skimp, and call it efficiency.

We need to learn a lesson from Bazalgette about doing a job properly.

Stop thinking under-spec and start thinking over-spec.

PUBLISH OR BE DAMNED

In 1963, John Kennedy Toole wrote *A Confederacy of Dunces*.

It was not a conventional novel.

He sent it to a publishing house he admired, Simon & Schuster.

The editor in charge felt it needed serious changes.

He wrote to Toole:

'More work is required. The various threads must be strong and meaningful *all the way through* – not merely episodic and then wittily pulled together.

In other words, there must be a point to everything you have in the book, a real point, not just amusingness that's forced to figure itself out.'

John Kennedy Toole tried to make the changes.

For two years he tried to rewrite his book to please the publisher.

But nothing he did was good enough.

Eventually the publisher wrote to him:

'There is another problem: with all its wonderfulness the book does not have a reason, it's a brilliant exercise in invention, but it isn't *really* about anything. And that's something no one can do anything about.'

That was the end as far as the publishers were concerned.

John Kennedy Toole became depressed and began drinking heavily.

No one would publish *A Confederacy of Dunces*.

And in 1969, aged 31, he committed suicide.

Years later, his mother found the abandoned manuscript on top of a cupboard in his bedroom.

She decided to try to fulfil her son's wish to get it published.

Over the next five years she sent it to seven publishers.

Each one turned it down.

No one would publish *A Confederacy of Dunces*.

Finally, in 1976, she found an author who was teaching at the local university.

His name was Walker Percy.

She asked him to read the book; he refused.

She begged him to read the book; he refused.

She badgered him to read the book until, eventually, just to get rid of her, he agreed to read it.

He was hoping that it would be so bad that he could stop after the first page.

But it didn't turn out like that.

'I started to read, I read on. And on. First with the sinking feeling that it was not bad enough to quit, then with a prickle of interest, then a growing excitement, and finally an incredulity; surely it was not possible that it was so good.'

And he realized this book was truly different.

Now Walker Percy also felt that the book must be published.

And for three years he wrote, and phoned, and met, and pestered everyone he could think of.

And everyone turned him down.

No one would publish *A Confederacy of Dunces*.

Eventually, in 1980, seventeen years after it was first written, he managed to nag a small local publisher into printing 2,000 copies.

And, despite the tiny print run, people started to read it.

The very next year, in 1981, *A Confederacy of Dunces* won the Pulitzer Prize.

Probably the greatest award any book can win.

John Kennedy Toole's name now sits alongside other Pulitzer Prize winners: John Steinbeck, Ernest Hemingway, William Faulkner, Harper Lee, Saul Bellow, Norman Mailer, Philip Roth and John Updike.

Since its publication, *A Confederacy of Dunces* has sold more than two million copies worldwide and been translated into eighteen languages.

It is now recognized as a true masterpiece.

But the best and most ironic part of the story for me comes from the title of the book.

John Kennedy Toole took it from a line in an essay written by Jonathan Swift over 200 years earlier:

'When a true genius appears in the world you may know him by this sign, that the dunces are all in a confederacy against him.'

THINKING IS PAINFUL

A few years ago I read a story in the *Evening Standard*.

It concerned five sadists and five masochists.

The sadists had all been sentenced to imprisonment and the masochists had been given probation.

The reason for their imprisonment was this.

Every week or so the sadists and masochists would all meet up and go to someone's flat.

Once there, they'd pair off: one masochist to one sadist.

Sounds a pretty satisfactory relationship.

One who likes giving pain, one who likes receiving it.

During the course of the evening, the sadists would perform acts that gave themselves and the masochists pleasure.

Presumably the usual: whips, chains, handcuffs, canings and beatings.

But evidently it also went further.

One particular piece of evidence that still stands out in my mind is that the sadists liked to nail the masochists' scrotums to planks of wood.

And apparently the masochists enjoyed this.

Afterwards, everyone would clean themselves up.

Apply antiseptic cream as necessary.

Have a drink and a chat, and make arrangements for next week.

All very amicable.

Until the police turned up and raided the flat and found evidence of criminal assault.

They questioned the owner of the house who freely admitted the activities.

But since everything was between consenting adults in private, he didn't see why it was a problem.

The police arrested him and the other sadists.

What they had done constituted the official definition of criminal assault.

The fact that it was consensual didn't come into it.

The masochists came forward to give evidence that no crime had been committed against them.

They were willing participants.

At which point they were arrested as accomplices before and after the fact.

They had aided and abetted in the crime of assault.

According to the law, a crime had been committed and therefore charges must be made.

The fact that the masochists enjoyed it merely made them complicit in the crime.

Therefore they were also charged.

And the sadists all got prison terms and the masochists all got probation.

Isn't that strange?

When we take the true purpose of something, the law in this case, and twist it into something else.

Supposedly the purpose of modern civilization is that it protects people from being oppressed.

So we make a law to protect people from oppression.

So that people are free to express themselves.

But they find that in expressing themselves they are breaking the law.

So we enforce the law and the law becomes the oppressor.

My dad, who was a policeman, always told me he saw his job as enforcing 'the spirit of the law, not the letter of the law'.

In other words: use your brain.

But most of us don't use our brains on the job.

Instead we enforce the letter of the law.

There's no risk involved in sticking to the letter of the law.

If we stick to the letter of the law we don't have to think.

Because there's risk involved with thinking.

There's nowhere to hide if it goes wrong.

But real creativity often comes with risk.

So don't just blindly follow the words themselves.

Take a risk.

Think.

HERD THINKING

A few years ago, a plane crashed in Africa.

It was an internal flight from Kinshasa, the capital of the Democratic Republic of Congo, to a town called Bandundu.

The crash happened as the plane was coming in to land.

Twenty people on board, including the two pilots, were killed outright.

There was only one survivor, who was immediately taken to hospital.

No one could understand the reason for the crash.

The plane was modern and in good condition.

It was a Czech-made twin-engine turboprop Let L-410.

Weather and visibility were excellent.

The two pilots, Chris Wilson from England and Danny Philemotte from Belgium, were both qualified and experienced.

The wreckage was examined and everything was found to be in good mechanical order.

They couldn't find a single reason for the plane to crash.

Until.

They questioned the only survivor, who was recovering in hospital.

He explained what happened and it was something no one could ever have guessed.

He said one of the passengers had hidden a young crocodile in their duffel bag.

Because it was illegal they had to smuggle it on board.

All of the luggage was stacked at the rear of the plane, behind the passengers.

As the plane was coming in to land the young crocodile got loose.

The stewardess ran to the front of the plane to tell the pilots.

The passengers saw her running away from the crocodile and panicked.

They all ran after her.

All the weight shifted to the front of the plane and it went into a dive.

The pilot told everyone to get back.

But with the plane nose-down they couldn't climb back up the aisle.

The pilot couldn't pull the plane out of the dive.

The plane ploughed, at full speed, head first into the ground.

And 20 people died.

But the young crocodile lived, because it was in the rear.

It crawled off the plane and tried to escape into the bush.

But when a local saw it, he hacked it to death with a machete.

He didn't know it came off the plane.

So, without the survivor, no one would ever have known what caused the crash.

Because you wouldn't ever dream a crocodile would cause a plane crash.

Actually what caused it was panic.

The crocodile wasn't a fully grown, twenty-foot-long man-eater.

It was small enough to fit into a duffel bag.

The worst it could do was to give you a nasty bite.

And if you left it alone it probably wouldn't even do that.

But no one was thinking.

Everyone was just copying everyone else.

If other people are running away, we'd better do the same.

Because that's what people do.

They copy each other without thinking.

Herd mentality is a strong force.

It overrides logic, questioning, debate, reasoning, common sense.

Even though the evidence shows it often results in bad decisions.

Injury, death, injustice, wars, genocide.

Entire nations follow along because each individual fears being different, fears being left out, fears being ostracized.

That's why the time to resist is at the point you find yourself going along with conventional wisdom.

It's uncomfortable to be the outsider.

But the only opportunity you have to think is before you join the herd.

Once you've joined, it's too late.

WHEN THINKING GETS IN THE WAY

Sheryl Sandberg is Chief Operating Officer of Facebook.

She earns around $26 million a year.

One day, she was giving a talk about what women need to do to get to the top of their profession.

She said they needed to learn from men.

Not that men are smarter, they're not.

That's the problem.

She said it wasn't men who were holding women back.

It was women who were holding women back.

Women were smarter than men and that was the problem.

Women would listen more carefully to what was said.

Women would respond more thoughtfully.

Women would pay more attention, answer the question, solve the problem.

Men wouldn't do any of that.

Men weren't listening to anyone else.

Men were just concentrating on what they wanted.

And it worked.

Because it meant they weren't as restricted as women.

She said she had a first-hand experience of this.

She'd been giving a speech to a couple of hundred men and women.

After the talk she was chatting to one of the women.

She asked her what she thought of the speech.

The woman said, 'I learned I'm going to start putting my hand up even when I don't think it's right.'

Sheryl Sandberg asked her what she meant.

She said, 'See, you probably didn't even notice.

At the end of your talk you said you'd take questions.

So everyone, men and women, raised their hands.

After about 20 minutes, you said you'd only take two more questions.

So, after you'd taken two questions, the women all stopped raising their hands.

But the men kept putting their hands up and you kept on answering their questions.

The women obeyed the rules and didn't get their questions answered.

The men broke the rules and got their questions answered.

So that's what I learned.

I have to raise my hand even when I think it's wrong.'

And Sheryl Sandberg was gobsmacked.

Because she hadn't even noticed what she'd done.

She hadn't noticed what all the women present had done.

And she is a woman, and a champion of women's rights.

If *she* hadn't noticed, what chance did other women have?

No wonder men had more power.

They had more power because they didn't ask anyone else's permission.

They just went ahead and did what they wanted.

And they weren't as scared of being wrong as the women were.

For them, getting the result was more important than being right.

And that's what Sheryl Sandberg meant by the biggest problem for women being women.

The only thing stopping them is themselves.

They are too smart.

They listen out for all the rules.

They very carefully pay attention to every detail.

They worry about being correct.

And that, Sheryl Sandberg said, is the problem.

Something everyone can learn from.

It's not thinking.

It's over-thinking.

THERE ARE NO ATHEISTS AT SEA

The more of a ship you can see, the higher in the water it is.

The less of a ship you can see, the lower it is.

That's pretty simple.

If you own a ship, you make your money by transporting cargo.

The higher the ship, the less cargo it's carrying.

The lower the ship, the more cargo it's carrying.

That's pretty simple, too.

So in order to operate at your most efficient level you want

the ship to be as low in the water as possible.

That's how you make money.

That's fine when the ship is in a nice calm harbour.

But as soon as it leaves harbour the water isn't calm

anymore.

There are storms and the waves wash over the side of the

ship.

If the ship is too low, it gets swamped and flooded.

The ship sinks, the sailors drown.

If you own the ship this may not be a problem.

Because the ship's insured.

So either way you make money: insurance or cargo.

That's how it was in Britain in the nineteenth century.

Because of constant overloading of ships, sailors died while

ship owners got rich.

In 1871, for instance, 856 ships sank just off the coast of Britain and nearly 2,000 sailors drowned.

In fact, one in five sailors drowned at sea.

The sailors called them 'coffin ships'.

Just one look at how overloaded they were and you knew they'd sink.

But the law said that seamen couldn't refuse to sail in them.

If they did they were thrown in prison for desertion.

In 1871 alone, 1,628 sailors were in gaol for refusing 'coffin ships'.

In one case, two complete crews chose gaol over the ship.

Eventually the owners got a crew of boys under the age of 17 who were more likely to take any job.

The ship sailed, it sank in a storm and went down with all hands.

But who cared, the ship owners were making lots of money?

There was one man who cared. Samuel Plimsoll.

He fought for a safe loading line on all ships to be passed into law.

The problem was many Members of Parliament were ship owners.

They weren't going to vote to cut their profits.

Plimsoll even threatened the Prime Minister, Benjamin Disraeli:

'I charge the government that they are playing into the hands of murderers inside this house who continue the murderous system of sending men and rotten ships to sea.'

Plimsoll outraged Parliament by shaking his fist in the Speaker's face.

'I am determined to unmask the villains who send our seamen to their death.'

Eventually, after twenty years of fighting, Plimsoll won.

Now every ship must have a clearly visible safe-loading line painted on the hull.

A circle with a straight line across it, like the London Underground sign.

If it's not clearly visible above water, the ship can't sail.

It's called 'The Plimsoll Line'.

As Tony Benn said of Plimsoll,

'My experience is that when people come along with a good idea, in the beginning it is completely ignored. If they go on about it they are considered mad and possibly even dangerous. Then, when it is eventually recognized as a good idea, nobody can be found who does not claim to have thought of it in the first place.'

In my opinion, that three-stage process is true of any original idea.

ORSON CART

Orson Welles knew the studio didn't want him to direct the picture.

He was brilliant but difficult.

That was why he couldn't get any work in America.

He'd had to spend the last decade making films in Europe.

This was his first, and last, chance back in Hollywood.

All they'd trust him with was a cheap B-movie.

Welles knew his reputation, the studio even sent executives along to check up on him.

All they saw was rehearsing.

Rehearsing, and rehearsing, and rehearsing.

They didn't see him shoot a frame of film.

It got dark and still he rehearsed the crew and the actors.

Camera moves, choreography, dialogue, all at precise points.

The executives thought he'd finally gone mad.

They watched him rehearsing all through the night.

Then, as dawn came up, he wrapped the set.

The executives walked over to him.

They said, 'Well, Orson, you haven't changed. You've spent a day and a night rehearsing with a full crew and not got a single shot. Now you're three days behind schedule and this movie's already in serious trouble.'

Orson Welles said, 'Gentlemen, if you'd known what you were looking at, you've just seen one of the greatest single-shot takes in cinema history. And we are now a week *ahead* of schedule'.

And he walked off.

What he'd just shot was the opening sequence of *Touch of Evil*, which is now considered to be the greatest opening and the greatest continuous shot of all time.

Orson Welles took a B-movie and turned it into a classic.

In one shot, he did the following:

Open on a close-up of a man setting the timer on a bomb. Camera swings to reveal couple approaching. Man places bomb in car boot. Couple get into car and drive off. Camera swings up over town following their car. Car is stopped by traffic cop. A different couple (the stars) cross the road. The car with the bomb passes slowly. Both couples stop at Mexican border. Border guards talk to walking couple who reveal they are newlyweds. He is a cop who has just broken a drug ring. The car with the bomb slowly drives off. The walking couple kiss. The car explodes.

Welles had set up the entire plot in just the opening shot.

He'd done it brilliantly, in a way no one had seen before.

He'd done it with beautiful, dramatic black and white lighting.

He'd done it with incredible tension.

He'd created the shot that would be taught in every film class from then on.

But he also knew exactly what he was doing to the studio executives.

There was no point explaining all of this to them.

They wouldn't have understood or cared anyway.

They would have tried to stop him.

So the best thing was to ignore them and go ahead and do it.

If it worked, he'd be a star, and if it didn't, he was finished.

But that's always true, either way.

As Orson Welles said, 'Don't give them what they want. Give them what they never dreamed was possible.'

COULDA, WOULDA, SHOULDA

Jack Brabham was an Australian racing driver.

It was 1959 and he was in the lead in the last race of the season: the Sebring Grand Prix.

He was on the final lap when his car ran out of petrol.

It just rolled to a stop, that's that.

Most drivers would climb out the car, throw their helmet on the floor and storm off.

Jack Brabham didn't do that.

He did something Grand Prix racing had never seen.

He got out of his car and started pushing.

As every other driver roared past him he pushed half a ton of metal a quarter of a mile to the finish line.

Then he collapsed.

When they brought him round, he found he'd crossed the line in fourth place.

Which was enough to make him World Champion.

He didn't win by being the classiest driver in the best car.

He won by not giving up.

Not feeling sorry for himself and not bitching about his bad luck.

He won by doing what no one else would have done.

Thinking of what no one else would have thought of.

The rules said the car and driver have to cross the line.

The rules didn't say the driver had to be sitting in the car.

So Jack Brabham became World Champion by thinking beyond the rules.

The next year he became World Champion again.

One of the greatest drivers ever, Stirling Moss, said he once had a broken axle and couldn't start the race.

Jack Brabham gave him the axle from his spare car.

Even though he knew that Moss was a better driver.

Then Brabham got in front of Moss on the track and took every corner with two wheels on the verge.

Chucking stones and gravel into Moss's face and car.

Brabham won.

As Moss said, he was a gentleman off the track but a hard bastard on it.

Jack Brabham said he could build a better car.

Anyone can say that, the difference is that Jack Brabham actually did it.

In 1966, he not only won the World Championship for the second time, he won it in a car he'd built.

He not only beat every other driver, he beat every other car company.

No one else has ever done it, before or since.

The next year, his car won the Constructors' Championship again.

That year Brabham was criticized for being too old to race. He walked to the grid at the start of the Zandvoort Grand Prix wearing a long false beard and leaning on a walking stick.

Then he got into his car and beat all the best drivers in the world.

To win his third World Championship title.

So three times he beat every other driver in the world and twice he beat every other car company.

One of my favourite expressions is 'You can have what you want, or you can have your reasons for not having it.'

Jack Brabham chose not to have his reasons.

He did it all by being unreasonable.

PART FOUR

THE MESSAGE IS THE MEDIUM

APPROPRIATE LANGUAGE

General Patton's speech to the Third Army before D-Day is considered to be the most motivational speeches of all time.

It isn't a pretty speech.

It wasn't made to be reprinted in newspapers and read by civilians.

It was meant for soldiers.

Hard, tough, men whose dirty business was killing or being killed.

There's only one way to talk to people like that.

Not just a corny appeal to patriotism, that only works for politicians.

You talk to people in their own language.

He started like this:

'No bastard ever won a war by dying for his country.

You win a war by making the other poor dumb bastard die for his country.'

That got their attention.

Then he quickly got down to the actual business of how to survive, in simple, impactful, language:

'I don't give a fuck for a man who is not always on his toes.

There are 400 neatly marked graves in Sicily, all because one man went to sleep on the job.

But they are German graves, because we caught the bastard asleep before his officer did.'

It turns the usual fear-based threat on its head.

This is simple: kill, or be killed.

And this is powerful grown-up advice on how to survive in that situation.

Then he acknowledges that he knows they didn't come here to be heroes.

They just want to get it all over with.

He acknowledges that and turns it on its head:

'Sure, we all want to go home.

And the shortest way home is through Berlin and Tokyo.

I don't want any messages saying "I'm holding my position."

We're advancing constantly and we're not interested in holding anything except the enemy's balls.

We're not just going to shoot the bastards, we're going to rip out their living goddamned guts and use them to grease the treads of our tanks.'

Finally, he accepts his reputation for driving the men beyond what's reasonable to expect.

He turns it on its head to show how this will actually save their lives:

'There will be some complaints that we're pushing our people too hard. I don't give a damn about such complaints. I believe that an ounce of sweat will save a gallon of blood. The harder we push, the more Germans we kill.

The more Germans we kill, the fewer of our men will be killed. Pushing harder means fewer casualties.

I want you all to remember that.'

After that speech, Patton's Third Army went through Europe like a whirlwind.

They destroyed nearly 1,000 German tanks.

They killed over half a million enemy soldiers, and captured nearly a million more.

They built 2,500 bridges, captured 80,000 square miles of enemy-held territory and liberated over 1,000 cities and towns.

In an off-the-record interview, Patton explained to a journalist why he'd used the language he'd used.

Put simply, you talk to a soldier in a soldier's language:

'When I want my men to remember something important, to really make it stick, I give it to them dirty.

It may not sound nice to a bunch of little old ladies at a tea party, but it helps my soldiers remember it.

You can't run an army without profanity, but it has to be eloquent profanity.

An army without profanity couldn't fight its way out of a piss-soaked paper bag.'

What we can learn from Patton is that whether we're talking to school teachers, little old ladies, construction workers, pole dancers, Oxbridge dons, children or soldiers . . .

We have to talk to people in their own language.

WHEN EXECUTION BEATS STRATEGY

When I first got to New York I was 19.

I'd just left sleepy old London and arrived at the busiest,
hippest city on the planet.

I went down the subway and stopped dead.

There was a huge poster opposite me saying 'YOU DON'T
HAVE TO BE JEWISH'.

This was only a couple of decades after the war.

It felt more like anti-Semitic graffiti than advertising.

But underneath it was a picture of a Chinese man, smiling
and eating a sandwich.

And underneath that, a line that said 'TO LOVE LEVY'S, REAL
JEWISH RYE BREAD'.

On the one hand it could have been offensive, but on the
other hand it was actually fun.

I walked round the corner and there was the same poster
headline.

But with a smiling Native American eating a sandwich.

And next to it another poster with a little black boy eating a
sandwich.

Then a fat Irish cop eating a sandwich.

And it became clear.

This was turning advertising on its head.

Until then, all advertising showed attractive, white, crew-cut or ponytailed, blonde people with perfect teeth.

But the Levy's posters treated that as a hick-town stereotype.

This was NEW YORK, we don't go in for that hokey suburban stuff.

We've got the best, and the worst, of everything in the entire world, right here.

And everyone doesn't look the same.

This is the real world, not the fake, patronizing ad world.

And right then I knew I wanted to do advertising like that.

Many years later I heard the history of that campaign and there's a lesson there for all of us.

The man who owned Levy's bakery in Brooklyn asked Bill Bernbach to look at his advertising.

Bernbach asked him where he ran his ads.

The man said he advertised in the *Jewish Chronicle*.

Bernbach said, 'There's your problem.

You picked that paper because of its Jewish readership.

But most Jews are immigrants and they won't eat packaged rye bread, they'll buy it fresh from the bakery.

We have to find a new audience who don't currently eat rye bread.'

So that became the strategy, to sell rye bread to people who didn't normally eat rye bread: market growth not market share.

Now if us folks in advertising had been doing that today we'd have stopped there.

All Creative is allowed to do is execute the strategy.

So the ads would have featured attractive, white, crew-cut or ponytailed, blondes with perfect teeth, eating rye bread.

Because that's the execution of that strategy.

But Bernbach didn't stop at the strategy.

He knew the strategy is just about being right.

It isn't about getting NOTICED and REMEMBERED.

That's Creative's job.

Which is why Bernbach decided that, in New York, the alternative to Jewish wasn't white.

The alternative was: Chinese, Black, Irish, Native American, Japanese, Italian, Polish, Puerto Rican.

And visibility would come not from hiding what made New York different, but from celebrating it.

And that's what changed the Levy's campaign from being just another piece of clever strategy to something much bigger.

Levy's became the biggest-selling rye bread in the entire city.

Then the biggest-selling rye bread in the entire state.

Then the biggest-selling in the entire country.

The strategy makes the advertising right.

The execution makes it great.

BIG DATA V SMART DATA

A while back, a man went into a Target supermarket in Minneapolis.

He asked for the manager.

He said 'I find this offensive. Your store has sent this leaflet, personally addressed to my teenage daughter.

Coupons for maternity clothing, nursery furniture, baby clothes, baby milk, diapers.

My daughter is still in school, what are you trying to do, encourage her to get pregnant?'

It seemed like a mistake, so the manager apologized.

A week later the manager still felt bad, so he called the man to apologize again.

This time the man was sheepish.

He said, 'Ah, there have been some things happening at home that I didn't know about. My daughter actually was pregnant and she hadn't told us.'

How did that happen?

How did Target's mailing system know the daughter was pregnant before she even told her parents?

Like most stores, Target has an enormous amount of information on its customers' purchases.

But none of that data is useful unless you know what to do with it.

So, in 2002, Target hired a statistician called Andrew Pole.

Most customers' shopping habits are well-formed and hard to change.

The only time they are vulnerable is during lifestyle changes.

Graduating college, moving house, changing jobs, marriage or divorce.

And the biggest lifestyle change of all is having a baby.

If a store can get pregnant customers to buy their baby goods, they'll buy everything else there too, just for convenience.

But if they wait until the baby is born, it's too late.

Because they'll be bombarded with offers from all the other stores.

So Target needed to identify pregnancies before anyone else.

Andrew Pole spotted twenty-five purchasing changes during the various stages of pregnancy.

For instance: around the third month, women switch from scented soap to scent-free soap.

Around the fourth month, they begin buying calcium, magnesium and zinc supplements.

Around the eighth month, they begin buying large packs of cotton balls and hand sanitizers.

But this specific targeting created a problem.

Women began to feel uneasy about Target knowing so much about their private life.

They felt they were being spied on.

And this is where big data needed creative marketing.

Andrew Pole disguised the contents of the leaflets they sent out.

They would still be full of baby goods, but now there was a lawnmower next to the diapers and a wineglass offer next to the baby clothes.

Lots of irrelevant offers among the baby goods.

Now the women didn't think they were being spied on.

Now they thought they'd spotted what they wanted in a leaflet full of lots of other money-off offers.

They weren't interested in the other offers, but that didn't matter.

They were just there to disguise the real offers.

Thanks to Pole's statistical analysis, Target sales increased by 50%.

From $44 billion when he was hired in 2002, to $67 billion by 2010.

Because what's better than big data is smart data.

THE MESSAGE IS THE MEDIUM

In 1977, Brian Clough was manager of Nottingham Forest.
They'd just been promoted into the First Division, the
equivalent of the Premiership at the time.
Clough's assistant was Peter Taylor and both of them wanted
to buy the Stoke City goalkeeper, Peter Shilton.
They'd built Forest into a team that could score goals.
Now they needed someone to stop them conceding.
If they could persuade Shilton to come, they'd be unbeatable.
But he was dragging his feet.
He wasn't sure Forest was a big enough club.
Taylor wanted to drive straight over to Stoke and talk the
reluctant Shilton into signing.
But Clough said no.
Clough said, let's wait a week.
Taylor asked, why, what difference will a week make?
Clough said, 'Look at it this way.
Shilton knows he's the best goalkeeper in England.
But he can't get into the England team because of Ray
Clemence.
Clemence plays for Liverpool, and Liverpool's winning
everything, so people think Clemence is better.

Shilton knows he can only show he's the best if he gets to play on a good team.

He doesn't think Nottingham Forest are big enough.

But currently he's playing for Stoke, in the Second Division.

And look at the fixtures list that's just come out.

Next week Stoke are playing Mansfield Town.

Mansfield bloody Town!

You couldn't even find it on a map.

And even if you could, can you imagine a wet, muddy Saturday in a tiny, rusty stadium with draughty changing rooms, damp towels and no showers?

And the crowd made up of one man and his dog.

Imagine what that'll feel like to the man who knows he should be playing in massive international stadiums.

He knows he won't get a chance as long as he's sitting in Mansfield Town's tatty, rickety changing room.

He'll feel depressed and desperate.

So let's wait a week, until after the game, then make him an offer.'

And that's exactly what they did.

And Peter Shilton nearly bit their hand off.

Nottingham Forest may have only just been promoted, but they were a damn sight better than Stoke and Mansfield Town.

And Clough and Taylor were right.

He was the missing piece.

Taylor had been a goalkeeper himself, so he always knew how good Shilton was.

Shilton commanded the entire area around the goal.

It gave the whole team the confidence to go forward and score.

And Clough, who'd been a centre forward, knew exactly how intimidating Shilton was for opposing strikers.

Clough said, 'Even if you get past the midfield and the defence, you've still got Shilton in front of you.

That's like a bank robber getting past the police and the security guards only to find the bloody bank vault welded shut and bricked up.'

And it was.

In his first season, Shilton kept an amazing twenty-three clean sheets. With Shilton in goal, Nottingham Forest did the incredible. They won the league, beating every team in England. The next year they did the unbelievable.

They won the European Cup, beating every team in Europe.

The year after, they did the impossible.

They won the European Cup again.

No English team, before or since, has done it.

And Peter Shilton went on to replace Ray Clemence as England's first-choice goalkeeper.

We can learn a great lesson from Brian Clough.

It's not just what you say that's important.
It's also where, and when.

YOUR IDEA NEEDS TOOTHPICKS

Two young men posed as restaurateurs.

They went to one of the most popular food expos in Europe.

It was full of 'high-end food experts'.

The two young men prepared the food for tasting by the experts.

They told everyone their food was an organic competitor to fast-food restaurants such as McDonald's.

But the two young men weren't actually restaurateurs at all.

They were filmmakers.

They had bought the food at McDonald's on their way to the expo.

Their problem was how to disguise it in front of these experts.

In the end it wasn't difficult.

All they needed was toothpicks.

They cut the Big Macs and Chicken McNuggets into small pieces then stuck a toothpick into each piece.

Then they placed the pieces, on toothpicks, on plates.

That's it.

And it worked.

The 'high-end food experts' took the toothpicks, they savoured the samples.

In 'high-end' food language they said it was 'nice and firm, it had a good bite.'

They took another toothpick.

They said, 'It rolled round the tongue nicely, like a fine wine.'

They said it had 'a rich taste, a warm release in the mouth'.

They took another toothpick.

They said it was 'fresh, with a good structure, not sticky'.

They said it was 'tasty, softer, more moist'.

The two 'restaurateurs' asked them to be specific.

To compare it directly to McDonald's.

The 'high-end food experts' took another toothpick and savoured each sample.

They said it was 'more pure than McDonald's, you can tell'.

They said it had 'a lot more taste than McDonald's, absolutely'.

They took another toothpick.

They said, 'It tastes better because organic is a good thing.'

They said, 'It's better for you, which is why it has a richer taste.'

They took another toothpick.

They said, 'It's a pure organic product, and that's what makes it very tasty.'

So the food was a success.

Or rather the toothpicks were.

Imagine if the food had been presented the way it's actually eaten.

In a bun, wrapped in tissue paper, with a McDonald's logo.

Do you think the 'high-end food experts' would have said the same?

The presentation changed what they thought.

They were tasting the presentation, not the food.

And that's where we go wrong in presenting our ideas to 'high-end' experts.

We don't allow for how much they'll be influenced by the presentation.

So if you want your idea to get bought, remember that.

Don't expect it to be judged purely on what you think are its merits.

Work out beforehand how you can get it taken seriously and judged in their world, in their language.

Not in the language of the world it actually has to work in.

Present your idea on toothpicks.

THE LADY WITH THE CHART

Florence Nightingale was born in 1820.

At that time women weren't allowed to go to university.

It would be a waste, their job was to marry, then look after their husband and children.

But Florence Nightingale's father thought differently.

Not being able to send her to university, he educated her at home.

First he taught her to read and write.

Then he taught her history, philosophy, Latin, Greek and, most unusually, mathematics.

Florence was an attractive young woman and had several offers of marriage.

But she didn't accept any of them.

Instead, during the Crimean War, she took medical training.

Then she formed and trained a unit of thirty-eight volunteer nurses.

And in 1854 she took them to the war.

What Florence Nightingale found at the military hospital horrified her.

Wounded soldiers were dying in droves.

Death in war is to be expected, but ten times more men were dying from disease than from battle wounds.

Typhus, typhoid, cholera, dysentery and malaria killed over 4,000 soldiers in her first year working in the hospital.

Most of it caused by defective sewers, malnutrition, overcrowding and lack of ventilation.

As an educated woman, she decided to change things.

She came back to London to lobby Parliament.

But she knew that whatever she wrote, most MPs wouldn't bother reading it.

It would be too long and detailed for them and their civil servants.

She was an intelligent woman.

She knew her audience.

She needed to show facts and figures, but she needed more than that.

She needed impact.

She needed communication.

She needed persuasion.

So Florence Nightingale argued her case using information graphics.

The basic pie chart had been invented fifty years before.

But if she hadn't been taught mathematics she wouldn't have known about it.

Florence Nightingale invented a more detailed form of pie chart.

A simple visual presentation of facts linking deaths to their causes in a way anyone could understand.

It was so powerful that it swept through Parliament like a bolt of electricity.

Brunel was briefed to design a new hospital immediately.

The staff were trained according to Florence Nightingale's methods.

And the death rate was cut from 42% to 2%.

Thousands of men lived who otherwise would have died needlessly.

Thanks to Florence Nightingale, the Crimean War was the last war in which more British soldiers died from disease than enemy action.

Mainly because she was an intelligent woman.

Mainly because she understood her audience.

Mainly because of her powerful, simple, graphic presentation of data.

It's not enough to have to have the right statistics, the best strategy, the correct marketing.

You have to have the best way to present them.

PART FIVE

DISASTER IS
A GIFT

DISASTER IS A GIFT

John Lloyd is a TV and radio producer.

One of his first shows was *The News Quiz* on Radio 4.

Then he co-wrote the radio scripts for *The Hitchhiker's Guide to the Galaxy*.

Next he produced *Not the Nine O' Clock News*.

Then *Spitting Image*.

Then *Blackadder*.

He was the originator of *Have I Got News For You*.

Now he produces and writes *QI*.

That's an incredible body of work for one person.

Once, a presenter asked him if any of this had been a struggle.

John said obviously it had been a struggle.

Consisting of fallouts, multiple sackings and missed opportunities.

He became depressed, wondering why he was always starting great projects, then getting fired from them by the people he worked with and respected.

John said this was his pattern in life, and it depressed him.

Until he came to realize that, actually, what seemed like disaster each time was actually opportunity in disguise.

So John's mantra became 'disaster is a gift.'

He wouldn't have done nearly so much with his life if he hadn't been fired so many times.

He'd have just stayed where he was.

But each time they let him go, it meant he was forced to start something new again.

So that each disaster was actually an opportunity in disguise.

Then he told a story about his father.

He'd been a captain in the navy during the war, in charge of three motor torpedo boats.

These were small, fragile, extremely fast boats, made out of plywood and driven by massive engines.

Their job was to use their speed to get as close as possible to bigger ships.

Then drop their torpedoes and get away fast.

Their speed was their only defence.

One day in 1942, John's father was returning from an overnight raid against the German-held coast of Europe.

Everyone was so exhausted, the lookout mistook the cliffs of Dover for a cloud formation.

All three motor torpedo boats drove at full speed up onto the beach.

John's father thought it was a disaster and the end of his career.

In the event, it wasn't held against him.

But if those boats had been serviceable he would have been sent on another mission immediately.

He would have been sent to stop the channel dash by the German battleships *Scharnhorst* and *Gneisenau*.

The Germans had caught the British completely by surprise and sent two massive battleships up the English Channel.

They were protected by another seven warships, forty motor torpedo boats and nearly three hundred aeroplanes.

British high command panicked and sent out whatever they had.

This consisted of six old Swordfish, fabric and wood, biplane torpedo bombers.

All six were easily shot down and thirteen men died in what was virtually a suicide attack.

If John's father hadn't run aground the day before, his boats would certainly have been sent out on a similar suicide attack.

John's father would have suffered the same fate as the Swordfish crews.

And John would never have been born.

So for John, his mantra 'disaster is a gift' was true even before he was born.

PLAN B

Jean Reinhardt was a gypsy.

He was born in 1910 in a camp outside Paris where he heard music being played round campfires.

As he grew, he learned the gypsy sound: guitar, banjo and violin.

He had no training, he just copied the older men.

But by thirteen he was able to make a living playing music.

By eighteen he was making enough money to get married.

He and his wife moved into a small wooden caravan.

She made cellophane flowers and the caravan was full of them.

One night, someone knocked over a candle.

Cellophane is incredibly flammable and within seconds the wooden caravan was blazing.

Reinhardt dragged his wife to safety, but was badly burned down the whole left side of his body.

So badly burned, the hospital doctors wanted to amputate his leg.

When he heard this, Reinhardt dragged himself out of the hospital.

Over the next year he exercised non-stop, and was able to walk again.

But whatever he did, two of the fingers on his left hand were paralysed and couldn't be straightened.

They were useless for playing.

So that was the end of his musical career.

Except at that point, around 1930, American jazz reached France.

This was a sort of music no one had heard before.

It tore up all the old rules and created a totally new sound.

When he heard it, something clicked in Reinhardt's head.

If jazz could tear up the rules, he could tear them up too.

He didn't have to play like everyone else.

He gave up the banjo and violin and concentrated on the guitar.

Only having two fingers on his left hand forced him to play with a unique style.

It didn't sound like traditional playing, but that was a good thing not a bad thing.

He brought this style to jazz, and added the gypsy sound he'd grown up with.

What resulted was the first jazz music outside the African American tradition.

If jazz was new, this was the newest kind of jazz.

He formed a group with violinist Stéphane Grappelli.

It was called the 'Quintette du Hot Club de France'.

They woke up European music and so Reinhardt became known by his gypsy nickname.

The Romany word for 'wake up' is Django: he was Django Reinhardt.

He is regarded as one of the greatest jazz guitarists of all time.

He invented a totally new guitar technique.

His band is considered one of the most original bands in the history of recorded jazz.

All because he lost the use of two fingers.

All because he couldn't play like everyone else.

All because he saw that as an opportunity instead of a problem.

And the opportunity is always to be creative.

What do you do when events don't go to plan and you can't change the events?

You change the plan.

A BRAND TO BANK ON

In 1904, Amadeo Giannini spotted a gap in the market.

Many poor Sicilians seeking a new life had emigrated to America.

Some stayed in New York, but the poorer ones, the hard-working fishermen, wanted to escape the crime.

They went to San Francisco.

Giannini knew these men, he understood them: they worked hard, they saved their money.

He knew they needed a bank to keep their money safe.

But no such thing existed for Sicilian immigrants.

Banks were just for rich White Anglo-Saxon Protestants (WASPs).

And that was the gap in the market Amadeo Giannini saw.

The gap for a bank where Sicilians would feel welcome.

He didn't know anything about 'branding' but he knew the name should be something they trusted.

He opened a little shop front with a big sign outside: BANK OF ITALY.

That told the Sicilian fishermen: this is your bank, it's not just for rich WASPs.

And the Sicilian fisherman deposited their savings. The Bank of Italy became a success.

But in 1906, San Francisco was destroyed by an earthquake.

All the buildings were flattened, there were riots and looting.

Giannini made his way through the mob on a horse and cart carrying crates of oranges.

As a fruit-seller, no one paid any attention to him.

What they didn't know was that hidden under the oranges was every penny of the bank's assets.

Giannini knew that as long as he had the money he still had a bank.

He went down to the docks where the fishermen worked.

He re-opened 'Bank of Italy' there, just a plank across two barrels.

His customers needed to borrow money to rebuild their homes and businesses.

He asked how much they needed.

When they told him, he said, raise half yourself then I'll lend you the other half.

This would prove they were serious and capable.

He was always proud that every penny was repaid.

Bank of Italy grew and grew until it became the only state-wide bank across California.

Now it was time to stop being a bank just for Sicilian fishermen.

He needed a brand that the all US citizens could feel was their bank.

Amadeo Giannini needed to rebrand.

In 1930, he changed the name to BANK OF AMERICA.

Now it felt like it had stature, it felt like it had history and tradition.

And Giannini was right about the rebranding.

Bank of America grew so fast that, in a few decades, it would become the second-largest bank in the entire USA.

One of the largest banks in the world.

In 1958 they launched the world's first credit card.

It was called the BankAmericard.

It created the credit-card market around the entire world.

Which meant that now it wasn't just a credit card for Americans.

So it needed rebranding again.

It needed a name to underline the freedom the card gave everyone to travel with their money anywhere.

BankAmericard was renamed VISA.

Today VISA has 38% share of the world's credit-card market.

It handles 62 billion transactions a year, amounting to $4.4 trillion.

Proving what Amadeo Giannini knew all those years ago.

Your best advertising is your brand.

CREATIVITY STARTS WITH A BRIEF

In 1929, Alfred Butts was an architect.

In 1930, he was unemployed.

The Depression hit the entire world, it was many times bigger and worse than any subsequent recession.

Like a lot of unemployed creative people, Alfred Butts needed an outlet for his creativity.

Even if he didn't have a job, he needed to be doing something.

He thought he'd like to invent a game.

But he didn't just start creating on a whim, he knew he needed a brief.

And this is the part of the story that I admire most.

He did his own research and wrote his own brief.

He carefully analysed the games market.

Obviously there's no money to be made inventing card games that can be played with the existing fifty-two-card pack.

Because everyone already has a pack.

No, whatever game he invented would have to require buying new pieces.

So he listed all the existing games.

He found he could group them into three main categories.

1)   Games that depended on chance and numbers, like bingo or dice.

2) Games that depended on skilful moves, like chess or draughts.

3) Word games that depended on knowledge, like anagrams or crosswords.

Many games combined the first two categories with varying degrees of chance and skill.

Backgammon, for instance, featured a fairly even combination of chance and skill.

Alfred Butts saw the opportunity.

The gap in the market.

A competitive word game that was a combination of chance and skill.

So he set about inventing one.

There needed to be a way that better players could beat weaker players.

Again, he did the research himself.

Every day, he carefully studied the front page of the *New York Times*.

He added up how often every single letter was used.

And he gave the letters a value according to the frequency of their use.

For instance, 'e' was the most common letter, therefore the easiest to use, so it should have the lowest score.

The letters 'b' and 'h' were less common, therefore they should have a higher score.

The letters 'q' and 'z' were hardly ever used, so they must be the most difficult and should have the highest score.

Alfred Butts began cutting up little wooden tiles and writing a large letter on each one, plus a smaller number indicating value.

And he called the game 'Lexico'.

He tried to get the major games manufacturers interested but they all turned him down.

There was no precedent for this kind of game.

He sold a few sets himself but by 1934 he had sold just eighty-four sets.

He changed the name to Criss Cross Words.

He began refining his initial idea.

He added a board, with different values on different squares.

And blank tiles that could be substituted for any letter.

But still, without advertising or distribution, hardly anyone knew about the game.

They say luck is when preparation meets opportunity.

That's what happened to Alfred Butts.

In 1952, Jack Straus, President of Macy's Department Store, was on holiday nearby.

At the hotel he played Alfred Butt's game, which was by now called Scrabble.

When he got back to New York he immediately placed a massive order.

With Macy's involved, the game had all the distribution and advertising it could ask for.

Alfred Butts's game began selling 6,000 units a week.

Today, two million Scrabble sets are sold every year in twenty-nine languages.

It's sold in boxed sets, deluxe editions, pocket sets, magnetic travel sets and for the visually handicapped, it's sold in large format type or even Braille.

You can play Scrabble online, on Facebook, on a video-game console.

There's a TV game show and even a World Scrabble Championship.

Alfred Butts knew discipline isn't the enemy of creativity. Discipline facilitates creativity.

BANGS FOR YOUR BUCK

In 1940 the British Army had escaped from Dunkirk, but they left all their weapons on the beaches.

An army can't fight without weapons, they needed guns in a hurry.

Here was one instance in which getting the brief right was crucial.

If the brief had been for well-designed, well-made weapons it would have taken years to manufacture.

Britain didn't have the time.

A brief for high-quality, durable weapons would have cost a fortune.

Britain didn't have the money.

So the brief was very clear: fast and cheap.

We need guns, we need lots of them and we need them now.

And so the design wasn't deliberated over by a group of experts who considered various options that were researched exhaustively.

One man sat at his kitchen table and designed the gun.

He designed it from parts that were easily available.

He designed it from material that was cheap.

He designed it so it could be made by anyone.

It was called the Sten gun.

It could fire the ordinary 9mm rounds the average pistol used.

It was made from stamped metal which could be punched out on a press or shaped with a hammer.

It was made from the exhaust pipe used on most cars.

From nuts and bolts you could buy in the local ironmonger's shop.

The mainspring was made by a bed-spring manufacturer.

It had just forty-seven parts and could be built in a shed.

It cost just over £2, which was an average week's wages.

It was so cheap and easy to make that the main manufacturer was the Tri-ang toy company.

They switched overnight from making tin toys to making the gun.

By the end of the war, four million Sten guns had been made.

They were sold everywhere in the world.

That's what real creativity is: Form *Follows* Function.

It's not just making something attractive that wins awards.

It's solving a problem in an unexpected and innovative way.

At the same time they needed guns, Britain also needed a new bomber.

Slow, heavy British bombers were being shot down at an alarming rate.

There was no metal to spare to make a new plane.

So de Havilland, one of Britain's aircraft companies, didn't use metal.

They made the entire plane out of what was easily available: wood.

Spruce, birch, mahogany, plywood and even balsa wood.

The plane was mainly built by furniture manufacturers, like Parker Knoll. They were the companies that had experience bending and shaping all sorts of wood.

The plane had two Spitfire engines and it was the fastest bomber of the war.

Because it was made from wood, it was so light it travelled at 400 miles per hour, faster than most Luftwaffe fighters.

It was so light it could fly six miles high and carry over a ton of bombs.

It was called the Mosquito, and nearly 8,000 were built during the war.

It cost just one fifth of what a Lancaster cost to build.

And the crews loved it because it had a much longer life expectancy.

That's what real creativity is: Form *Follows* Function.

It's not just making something attractive that wins awards.

It's solving a problem in an unexpected and innovative way.

Winston Churchill summarized real creativity best:

'We have no money, we shall have to think.'

STUDENTS ARE CUSTOMERS TOO

In 2012, Emma Sulkowicz was raped in New York.

But not on the streets of Harlem.

She was raped in her bed, in her bedroom, in her dormitory, in her university.

The place where she should have been safer than anywhere else.

She was a freshman art student at Columbia University.

Of course, she reported the rape to the university authorities.

Two other students reported it with her.

But the university authorities didn't do anything.

So she reported the rape to the local police.

But the police didn't do anything either.

At American colleges, cases of rape are usually treated as high spirits among young men.

Especially if the young men are in a fraternity or on the college football team.

It isn't really seen as rape, as such.

Not in a nasty way.

It was probably just some drunken partying that got out of hand.

This stuff happens at college, get over it.

But Emma Sulkowicz didn't want to get over it.

She tried for two years to get something done, but the university ignored her.

So she decided to get their attention.

She decided to make it her final art project.

The piece would be called CARRY THAT WEIGHT.

Until she graduated she would carry her mattress with her wherever she went.

To classes, to the cafeteria, to the shops, to the bathroom.

Dragging it through the halls and across campus, 24/7.

Whenever anyone asked her what she was doing, she'd tell them.

The mattress was the place she was raped.

The mattress symbolized the emotional weight she must carry around for the rest of her life.

The mattress symbolized the way the university ignored the rape as if it was her problem, not theirs.

And soon every young woman on campus wanted to join in.

Wherever she went there was a crowd of young women wanting to help her carry the mattress.

And the art piece grew to be a website, with dozens of young women signing up to participate.

And then an event, a gathering of hundreds of young women bringing their own mattresses.

The event was called: CARRYING THE WEIGHT TOGETHER.

The call-to-action said 'No one should carry this weight alone as we are all affected by sexual violence and rape culture at our university.'

And like any large, controversial gathering it quickly got picked up by the papers, magazines, Internet, TV stations.

Not just across New York State, but across America and, with the story spreading online, across the world.

Which means Columbia University is now getting a nationwide reputation for having a rape culture.

And parents will avoid sending their daughters to the college with a reputation for a rape culture.

And, given that half the students at Columbia are female, that will jeopardize 50% of its entire income.

And that is when you get the attention of the university authorities.

Because that is when the board of governors steps in.

Sadly, not for moral reasons but for financial ones.

It didn't matter, Emma Sulkowicz finally got a result.

Because she created a controversy that grew and grew until it took on a life of its own.

Until it couldn't be ignored.

IF IT'S BROKE DON'T FIX IT

Manuel Francisco dos Santos was Brazilian.

He was born with a deformed spine.

He also had one leg curved outwards that was 6cm shorter than the other. Most parents, myself included, would try to fix the problem.

We'd have therapy and surgery on the child's spine and legs.

We try to get them straightened, lengthened, corrected.

Maybe the child could learn to walk as well as ordinary people.

But dos Santos's parents couldn't afford that.

He was just left to grow up, like any other Brazilian street kid.

Which meant he played a lot of football.

As he grew, he found the shorter leg gave him an unusual running style.

The other kids couldn't tell what he was about to do.

They'd think he was going one way but he'd go the other.

Playing against him was like trying to catch smoke.

He eventually became a national hero known as 'Garrincha'.

Everyone knows that Pelé was the best football player ever.

Everyone outside Brazil that is.

Because the people inside Brazil who remember seeing Garrincha play say he was even better than Pelé.

He won the World Cup twice with Brazil, in 1958 and 1962.

He scored 244 goals in 648 games.

Brazilians called him 'Anjo de Pernas Tortas', the 'Angel with bent legs'.

In 1958, in a game against Italy, he beat four Italian defenders and the goalkeeper.

Then in front of the open goal he stopped.

He turned around and waited for another defender to catch up. When he did, he beat him and finally rolled the ball into the net.

In the 1962 World Cup against Spain, he dribbled past a defender and stopped.

Again, he waited while two more defenders caught up.

Then he dribbled past both of them and put in an inch-perfect cross for his own forward to score.

Four times he scored straight from a corner kick with his 'banana shot'. When he retired, he was nearly forty years old and a grandfather.

Over 130,000 people came to watch his final match.

He was a hero.

All because he didn't try to fix a disadvantage.

He turned it into an unfair advantage.

PART SIX

THE VALUE OF IGNORANCE

A FORMULA TO AVOID THINKING

A Spanish woman won the lottery.

An immense amount of money, around €100 million.

She was interviewed by all the media.

They wanted to know the usual.

How did she feel, how would it change her life, who would she give large chunks of cash to?

But the part that interested me was how she picked the numbers.

They asked her, what was her system?

She said she was truly blessed.

To prove it, she carefully went through all the numbers with the interviewer.

She had used all her family's birthdays.

Someone up there was looking after her because they all came up.

Every single one.

What the interviewer found more interesting was the date of her birthday: 7 July.

She said yes, the seventh day of the seventh month.

7 times 7 is 48, so that was one of her winning numbers: 48.

The interesting part, for the rest of us, is that 7 times 7 is not 48.

7 times 7 is 49.

She got it wrong.

If she'd got it right, she wouldn't have won.

But the lady wouldn't accept it, her belief overrode the facts.

She was blessed and that was that.

And it reminded me of Dumbo's feather.

In the film, Dumbo's ears are so big he can use them to fly.

But he doesn't believe he can fly, so he can't.

The little mouse realizes there's no point in giving him a logical explanation about flight.

So he gives him a feather and tells him it's magic.

As long as he holds the feather he can fly.

Dumbo tries it and of course it works, because it supplies the missing ingredient: belief.

Belief is what you've got when you haven't got knowledge.

Belief is what you've got instead of thinking.

Of course, eventually Dumbo finds he doesn't need the feather to fly.

That's how it works in Hollywood.

But in the real world everyone clings on to their beliefs.

Except we call them systems.

Systems we can learn and use without the difficulty of thinking.

We love them because there's security there.

We don't have to think.

Which means we don't have to take risks.

So we are very attached to these formulas.

The problem with formulas is they keep us locked in conventional wisdom.

We can't discover anything new as long as we stick to formulas.

We will be limited by conventional wisdom.

Rules such as this:

'The laws of aerodynamics prove that the bumblebee should be incapable of flight, as it does not have the capacity (in terms of wing size or beats per second) to achieve flight with the degree of wing loading necessary. The calculations are based upon a simplified linear treatment of oscillating aerofoils. The method assumes small amplitude oscillations without flow separation.'

My daughter recently showed me a quote concerning that particular piece of conventional wisdom:

'According to the laws of aerodynamics the bumblebee can't fly. But the bumblebee doesn't know that, so it just carries on flying around.'

STOP TRYING

As a youngster, football was Ian Wright's life.

He lived for it, spent all his waking hours playing it.

He knew he was going to be a professional.

As a teenager, he went on trials and gave them his everything.

He had a trial at Southend, but they turned him down.

He knew it was just about trying harder.

He had a trial at Brighton, but they turned him down.

He tried even harder.

Leyton Orient turned him down.

So he tried harder and harder.

Charlton turned him down.

Millwall turned him down.

Eventually he became disheartened.

He was into his twenties by now.

He couldn't try any harder, he'd given everything.

If he hadn't made it by now it was pretty clear he wasn't ever going to.

So he began working at a refinery in Woolwich.

It was dirty work.

But it was a regular job with regular money.

And he had a wife and child to support now.

He had to settle down and get real about what his responsibilities were.

But he still loved football.

So he played amateur football at the weekends with a club called Dulwich Hamlet.

One weekend a coach from Crystal Palace spotted him playing.

He wrote to him and asked him if he'd like to come along to the club for a trial.

Ian had already accepted that his football career was over so he wouldn't bother.

There was no point in starting all that again.

At his refinery job, he showed the letter to the guy who was in charge of his section, Garry Twydell.

Garry had been a professional footballer for a couple of years. He took a different view.

He said, 'This is your chance, Ian, you have to try. If you don't you'll never know and you'll always regret it.'

Ian said the trial was two weeks, he couldn't take that long off work.

He couldn't risk losing the job.

Garry Twydell said, 'Look, take a week off, say you've got family problems. Then another week sick leave. I'll back you up. You won't lose the job.'

And eventually he persuaded Ian Wright to take the time off work and go along to Crystal Palace for the trial.

Ian Wright expected the trial to go the way every other trial went.

But at least he had his job to go back to, so he could relax.

He stopped trying so hard.

He just enjoyed himself playing football for every minute of the next two weeks.

Like a holiday.

And an amazing thing happened.

With no pressure on him, just playing for the love of it, he was absolutely brilliant.

The trial went so well that Crystal Palace signed Ian Wright.

Long after he thought all chances had gone, he signed professional.

In his first season, he scored 24 goals.

In five years at Crystal Palace he scored 117 goals.

He was voted their 'Player of the Century'.

Then Arsenal, one of the biggest clubs in Britain, bought him for a club-record £2.5 million.

He scored 24 goals in his first season at Arsenal.

He was their top scorer for the next six years.

In 1997, he became Arsenal's highest-ever goal scorer.

During his time at Arsenal he won the Premier League.

He won the FA Cup twice.

He won the League Cup.

He won the European Cup Winners' Cup.

And in 2005 he was voted into the English Football Hall of Fame.

All because he gave up, and stopped trying so hard.

Stopped working at it and started to enjoy it.

THEY DON'T KNOW THEY DON'T KNOW

I heard a professional poker player being interviewed.

Over the course of her career, she'd won many millions of dollars.

She was asked about the secret of her success.

Was it learning to spot the other person's 'tell'?

She said, no, that was for amateurs.

The 'tell' was popularized in the movie *Casino Royale*.

James Bond says the trick is to watch the other player's facial expression.

They will always have an involuntary movement: a twitch, a raised eyebrow, a cough, a scratch, something they do involuntarily when they've got a great hand.

For James Bond, the secret was learning to read the other player, so their hand becomes like an open book to you.

The female professional player said that was nonsense.

And this is the brilliant part.

She said that all a 'tell' could reveal was what the other player thought about their cards.

Not the truth.

She said, early in her career, she had been playing against an opponent for a quarter of a million dollars.

She had learned to read his 'tell'.

She could see he thought he had a great hand, and she knew she didn't, so she folded.

But when the cards were revealed, he didn't actually have a great hand at all.

Her cards could have beaten his easily.

But he thought he had a great hand, and that made the difference.

She had folded to his opinion, not the facts.

She hadn't realized that she was a much better player and he had read the cards completely wrong.

That was the last time she ever placed any faith in the 'tell'.

Because it was just someone else's opinion.

From then on she always relied on the facts.

She always kept the numbers in her head.

She knew what cards had been played, what cards were left, so she knew exactly what the odds were.

She played the odds, not the other person.

She said that was why most people lost.

They treated it as a macho battle between human opponents.

Bluff and counter-bluff.

She'd learned the hard way that it was about playing the numbers, the percentages, the facts.

She'd learned that other people's opinions are just that.

Opinions. Not facts.

It's the same everywhere.

In any business meeting, any discussion about strategy, any presentation of thoughts, any review of work.

Other people may be more eloquent, they may be able to shout louder, they may be more plausible, even get more agreement.

All of that makes them appear confident.

And if we are impressed by their confidence, we begin to doubt.

We begin to believe that maybe they are right.

Because we see they are confident and we assume they know something we don't.

And we fold even when we shouldn't.

But what if their confidence is misplaced?

As it was with that poker player's opponent.

What if they aren't as good as us and they don't know what we know?

What if they're wrong?

Sometimes confidence comes from ignorance.

MOTIVATION

Bill Shankly took over as manager of Liverpool FC when they were in the Second Division.

He took a group of players and motivated them to win promotion.

He motivated them to fight their way up the First Division (the equivalent of the Premier League).

He motivated them to win the First Division.

He motivated those players to beat the best in England.

Then he motivated them to play against the best in Europe.

In 1965, they played in the European Cup against the champions of Germany: FC Cologne.

They played in Cologne and they drew.

They had the replay in Liverpool and they drew.

They had to play a deciding game at a neutral venue.

They played in Rotterdam and they drew.

Even after extra time they still drew.

After 400 minutes of football the game was decided on the toss of a coin, which Liverpool won.

The team came back to England, and three days later, they had to play Chelsea.

In the semi-final of the FA Cup.

And they were spent.

They sat in the dressing room before the Chelsea game, knackered.

Shankly stood and looked at the team.

He said, 'Lads, I've got something here I didn't want to show you in case it upsets you. But there's nothing to lose now, so I might as well.'

And he took a brightly coloured brochure out of his pocket and held it up.

He said, 'This is the leaflet that Chelsea have had printed for when they get to the final at Wembley.

They think tonight is a formality, because they think you're too knackered to win.

They think you left everything on the field in Rotterdam.

They think flying over there and playing the Germans took it out of you, so they think you're easy meat now.

That's why they've printed up their brochure for when they get to Wembley.

After the formality of brushing Liverpool aside.

What do you think, lads, is it a formality?

Can they just brush you lot aside?

Are you as knackered, as done in, as they think?

Are you finished?'

As he spoke, the players began to get irritated, then annoyed, then furious.

Chelsea thought they'd just brush Liverpool aside, did they?

Thought Liverpool would just roll over, did they?

And Shankly's team went out and ran the legs off Chelsea.

Liverpool won two–nil and knocked Chelsea out of the FA Cup.

After the match, Bill Shankly walked over to Chelsea's manager, Tommy Docherty, to shake hands.

Docherty was shell-shocked.

He said, 'Bill, how did they ever manage that? They've just come back from playing against the German champions in Rotterdam. How come they've got so much energy?'

And Bill Shankly handed him the Chelsea Cup Final programme.

He said, 'There you are Tom, a little souvenir.'

Tommy Docherty looked at it and said, 'What the fuck's this?'

He didn't recognize it.

He didn't recognize it because Chelsea hadn't printed it.

Bill Shankly had just the one copy printed to show his team before the match.

Just to motivate them a little bit.

THE DEATH OF LANGUAGE

ATSC stands for Advanced Tactical Security & Communications.

ATSC was a very successful British company.

They sold bomb detection equipment to the developing world.

Between 2008 and 2010 they sold nearly 1,500 of these detectors to Iraq alone.

Each unit cost around £40,000.

Iran spent approximately £52 million on this advanced equipment.

The bomb detectors worked on the principle of 'electro-magnetic ion attraction'.

Each unit was hand-held with a swivelling antenna which was attracted to any explosives.

The unit was fitted with 'programmed substance detection cards'.

These were similar to the chips in a mobile phone and could be changed depending on the particular substance you wanted to detect.

The chips utilized 'the proprietary process of electrostatic matching of the ionic charge and structure of the substance'.

Which was how it detected the different types of explosives.

Except it didn't.

The entire thing was a massive con.

The antenna was actually just a car aerial.

It was screwed loosely to the plastic handle so it would swivel as the user's hand moved.

The 'programmed substance detection cards' were the standard anti-theft tags you find on clothing in most stores. They cost two to three pence each.

The device had no battery and was supposed to work off the static electricity generated by the user.

Dr Markus Kuhn of Cambridge University said, 'It has no memory, no microcontroller, no way any form of information can be stored.'

The US Army tested them and found them absolutely useless. In one test, the device failed to detect a ton of explosives in a truck immediately behind the user.

A *New York Times* reporter drove his car through nine checkpoints while the arms and ammunition in the boot went undetected.

While these devices were in use by the Iraqi police and military, thousands of people died in undetected bomb blasts. But it wasn't just Iraq.

Six thousand units were sold to twenty countries including: Lebanon, Jordan, Saudi Arabia, Afghanistan, Pakistan,

Thailand, Algeria, Bahrain, Kenya, Bangladesh, India, Iran, Syria, Tunisia and the UAE.

Why did so many people fall for it?

We are all susceptible to 'pseudoscience'.

We don't question something if it has the credibility of technical-sounding language.

We don't interrogate the thing itself if the way it is presented is sufficiently obscure as to be beyond our grasp.

We are satisfied that it's been developed by people more knowledgeable than us.

So we don't question it.

Just like we don't question the proliferation of jargon in the business we work in.

We try to learn what it means.

Then we accept it as the conclusions of experts in that area.

And use it ourselves to sound more informed in meetings.

And, in doing so, we give it more credibility.

And so on.

James McCormick, the founder of ATSC, was sentenced to ten years for fraud.

He had another view of the equipment he sold, and the way he sold it.

He said, 'It did exactly what it was meant to do. It made money.'

A PIGGYBACK RIDE IN SPACE

In 1957, Russia launched Sputnik, the world's first satellite. America was stunned.

Sputnik passed over the USA every ninety minutes, sending out radio signals.

The USA couldn't shoot it down, they didn't have the technology.

The entire country was petrified.

American newspapers went into hysterics.

With a fleet of satellites, Russia could hit the USA whenever they wanted.

America, the world's most powerful country, was defenceless.

At that moment, the space race began.

For the next twenty years America would throw everything they had into beating Russia.

The world could see that Russia was the one country that the USA were scared of.

And Russia became a global superpower, alongside the USA.

But what was the Russian perspective?

At the end of the Second World War, Russia was broke, they could barely feed their own people.

They wanted to build a nuclear missile like the one America had.

But theirs was too big, too unwieldy, too slow to set up.

So the scientists decided to see if they could use it to launch something, anything, just to keep their jobs.

A crude metal sphere would do, but how would they know if it worked?

They had no radar that could see anything that far away.

The cheapest and easiest way was to fit a small transmitter inside the metal sphere, just sending out 'beep beep' signals.

So the Russian scientists sent up the little metal ball and listened for the 'beep beep' signals to confirm it worked.

Then they went off to the canteen and thought no more about it.

But the USA picked up the transmission too and they didn't know it was just an empty metal ball.

To them it was something out of science fiction, an immense threat.

When the Russian leader Khrushchev saw the American hysteria he immediately told the scientists to launch more 'firsts'.

Russia couldn't afford new missiles so they had to use what they had.

The missile that could just about get something up into orbit.

So they put the first living creature, a dog named Laika, into orbit.

Then they put the first man, Yuri Gagarin, into orbit.

Then they put the first woman, Valentina Tereshkova, into orbit.

Then they had a cosmonaut make the first ever spacewalk, in orbit.

All the Russians had was a missile that could just about achieve orbit.

But the Americans didn't know that.

The Americans didn't know what Russia was capable of.

And that scared them.

With each 'first' the Americans got more hysterical.

As they did, they cemented Russia's place in the world's mind as the USA's only real rival.

For Khrushchev, it was a classic piece of marketing.

He made America spend all those billions on advertising Russia.

The world believed America had an equal.

Which is how you want the market leader to respond to your campaign.

To needle them into spending their money on a campaign that advertises your brand.

In the public's mind it becomes a two-horse race.

Your brand is elevated into equality with the market leader.

And that's how, with hardly any money or resources, the

Russian 'space team' took market share from the brand leader.

Of course, America eventually won the space race.

With their vastly superior resources, they were always going to.

But Russia made sure the USA spent a hell of a lot of their money giving them a piggyback ride along the way.

PART SEVEN

QUESTION THE QUESTION

REINTERPRET THE BRIEF

Jerry Weintraub was a young concert promoter.

He'd finally managed to get the biggest break of his life.

He'd talked Elvis Presley into letting him promote a tour.

If the tour was a success, Weintraub was a success.

But if the tour was a failure, it was the end of his career.

Not only would he be broke, but word would spread.

No other act would ever let him promote them.

Elvis had only had one stipulation, 'I don't wanna see any empty seats in any of my shows.'

That sounded fair enough to Weintraub.

In fact, even before the tour started the seats for all the evening shows were sold out.

This made Weintraub wonder if he could sell some tickets for matinee concerts.

So he briefed the manager of the first venue to advertise a daytime performance.

On the morning of the show, Weintraub turned up at the manager's office.

He noticed a pile of tickets on the table.

The manager said a few hundred seats were unsold because it was a daytime performance.

Weintraub's life flashed before his eyes.

Elvis Presley was about to go onstage and see the one thing he'd said he didn't want to see.

Several hundred empty seats.

Weintraub thought it was the end of his career.

How the hell was he going to fill up the theatre with just hours to go?

Then he realized that filling the theatre wasn't the brief.

'I don't wanna see any empty seats' was the brief.

So Weintraub had workmen take out all the back rows at the theatre.

When Elvis came onstage all he saw was a packed theatre without a single empty seat.

The concert and the tour were the turning point in Weintraub's career.

He went on to become the biggest concert promoter in the US.

Many years later some environmental activists had a very different sort of problem in the Arctic.

Seal hunters were clubbing thousands of seal pups to death.

The pelts from the young pups made beautiful, soft sealskin coats.

The hunters just walked up and crushed their skulls.

The question for the activists was how to stop the killing.

There were too many hunters for them to stop them individually.

And the hunters were tough, violent men.

Then the activists realized the brief wasn't to stop the hunters.

The brief was to prevent the pups being killed.

They could ignore the hunters and remove the reason to kill the pups.

The activists went all over the Arctic with spray cans of paint.

They simply sprayed a splash of paint on every seal pup.

The pups didn't care, once it dried they didn't even know it was there.

But it ruined their pelts for making coats.

Now there was no point in the hunters killing seal pups because they couldn't sell the pelts.

Jerry Weintraub and the environmental activists discovered the same thing.

Real creativity doesn't come from struggling to answer a difficult brief.

Real creativity comes from getting upstream of the brief and finding a different answer.

Reinterpreting the brief is often solving the problem.

UPSTREAM MARKETING

In 1989, Trevor Baylis saw a TV programme about AIDS in
Africa.

It said the reason for the spread of AIDS was ignorance.

It said AIDS in Africa could only be countered by education
about the disease.

By letting the general population of Africa know the scale
and the cause of the problem.

But they couldn't do that unless they could find a way to
communicate with everyone.

And most people lived in villages that didn't even have access
to electricity.

So Trevor Baylis thought upstream of the problem.

Before you could address AIDS you needed to educate.

Before you could educate you needed to communicate.

Obviously, the easiest way to communicate at that time was
by radio.

But radios needed an electrical supply or batteries.

But there was nowhere, and no money, to buy batteries.

So the real problem was batteries.

If his reasoning was right, the block in communicating was
batteries.

So having reduced the problem to something he could
handle, he went to his shed and started inventing.

He thought the solution should work like a clock.

Wind it for a few seconds, the spring stores the energy and releases it slowly.

If he could convert manual energy into electrical energy, he'd have a radio that didn't need batteries.

His first prototype featured a small transistor radio, an electric motor from a toy car, and a clockwork mechanism from a music box.

And it worked.

He patented the idea and tried to get backers, but no one wanted to know.

Everyone he approached saw it as an eccentric idea without a market.

In the world where all the potential investors lived, all portable radios worked on batteries.

This invention was no more than a curiosity.

Eventually it occurred to Baylis that he was approaching the wrong people.

Before he could sell his invention, he needed to create a demand for it.

A demand among his target audience: investors.

People on the lookout for new and exciting ideas.

So again, he thought upstream of the problem.

Who would benefit from a radio that could be played absolutely anywhere in the world?

And he approached the BBC World Service.

The people who broadcast around the world: in the jungle, in the desert, on the ocean, in the Arctic.

And the BBC World Service said they'd love more people to be able to listen to their programmes.

So they contacted another part of the BBC.

They contacted BBC Television and suggested it as a story for their *Tomorrow's World* programme.

The weekly show about the future – inventions and innovations that would change our lives.

And they thought a radio that worked without batteries was just the sort of story for them.

The week after it was featured, Trevor Baylis was inundated with offers from investors eager to back his new invention.

Now it had been featured on *Tomorrow's World* it wasn't just some eccentric crackpot invention anymore.

Now it was the future of portable communications.

And investors competed with each other to offer more and more money for a share in it.

Trevor Baylis's radio went into production.

And now you can hear programmes on it, and information and education, anywhere in the world.

Because he knows how to get upstream, and change the problem from one you can't solve to one you can.

REDUCTIO AD ABSURDUM

Many years ago, I was at a seminar.

It wasn't an advertising seminar, but it was one of the most useful seminars I ever attended.

The main point of the seminar was that to be successful at anything you need to reduce your focus to one thing.

One thing.

That doesn't mean you can't *do* other things.

But it does mean you prioritize one thing.

Something we are all terrible at.

To demonstrate, the speaker asked if anyone was ready to make a declaration about their future.

One young man stood up straight away.

He said, 'I'm going to be the best actor in the world.'

Everyone cheered and he sat down.

The seminar leader asked him to stand up again.

The leader said, 'That's two things. Which one do you want?'

The young man said, 'Pardon? That's only one thing.'

The seminar leader said, 'No, that's two things. Which do you want?'

The young man said, 'I want to be the best actor. That's one thing.'

The seminar leader said, 'That's why you won't get what you want. You can't see that's two things.'

The young man said, 'How is that two things?'

The seminar leader said, 'Being an actor is one thing. Being "the best" is another thing.

They are separate targets.

If you want to be an actor, you may have to accept that you are not the best at it.

But if you love acting, that won't matter, because you will have spent your life doing what you love.

However, if you want to be "the best" then you need to find out what you are the best at.

The world will tell you that.

It may not be acting.

But if you want to be "the best" that won't matter.'

We were all very quiet.

The seminar leader said, 'Now your job is to sort out your priority, work out which you want to be.

Do you want to do a particular thing, a craft?

Or do you simply want to be the best?

When you've reduced it to one simple, powerful, unarguable target you will have a lot more chance of achieving it.

Because all your energy will be focused on that one thing, rather than split between two goals.'

Up until that point, I had always thought I wanted to be an art director.

I trained at art school for it.

Even though I wasn't great, that was what I wanted to be.

But people were telling me my ideas were much better than my layouts.

I realized I didn't want to be a second-best anything.

I wanted to be a first-best something.

So rather than being a second-rate art director, I switched to being a copywriter.

And it worked.

I got a job at Boase Massimi Pollitt and worked my way up to deputy creative director.

Eventually I wanted to be an executive creative director.

But everyone said I was a much better teacher.

But I didn't want to be a teacher.

So I opened my own agency, Gold Greenlees Trott, with an entire creative department of youngsters.

That way I could call myself executive creative director, but be a teacher.

And it worked.

That laser-like clarity of prioritizing what I wanted really worked for me.

It also worked in all the ads we subsequently did.

Every brief we received.

Every media plan.

Every client conversation.

It wasn't always comfortable, some suits, planners, clients hated it.

But usually it resulted in simple, powerful communication.

Instead of trying to cram several things into the brief.

It's better to succeed at one thing than fail at several.

A ROSE, BY ANY OTHER NAME

Have you ever wondered why Bank Holidays are called that?

After all, it isn't only the banks that get a holiday.

So is it because the holidays started with the banks?

Well, yes and no.

Sir John Lubbock was a Liberal MP.

He was a reformer who wanted to improve the lot of the working class.

Which, until that time, had been poverty and misery.

The Liberal party had already made some improvements:

Children under nine were no longer allowed to work.

Children under thirteen could only work six hours a day.

Children under thirteen also had to have two hours a day of schooling.

Women could work no more than ten hours a day.

But Sir John Lubbock wanted more.

He wanted something that was unheard of for poor people.

Holidays.

The only time they got off was Christmas Day and Good Friday.

Lubbock wanted them to have four more days throughout the year.

He chose: Boxing Day, Easter Monday, Whit Monday and the first Monday in August.

But this would never get through the House of Commons.

Most of the MPs, particularly the Conservatives, were landowners and industrialists.

The moneyed classes, who didn't see why the work-shy lower classes should get time off to laze around and do nothing but sleep and drink.

It could start a trend.

They would start wanting more and more time off for more and more pay.

Until it became impossible for the ruling classes to keep the factories open at a profit.

Giving the working class time off would be taking money straight out of their employers' pockets.

They'd never vote for it and Sir John Lubbock knew that.

But he also knew that the banks needed to close at various times during the year.

They needed to suspend transactions while they got their books in order.

And of course, because lots of the MPs were bankers themselves, they could understand that.

So John Lubbock presented his bill as The Bank Holidays Act 1871.

It went through Parliament pretty much on the nod.

Most of the MPs who would have voted against public holidays didn't even bother turning up to vote.

The Bank Holidays Act was passed.

The MPs had no idea how important this innocent sounding act was.

But Sir John Lubbock knew that if the banks were formally closed no business could be done.

A day off was inevitable for everyone.

And now it had passed into law.

Sir John Lubbock regarded it as his greatest political achievement.

He said, 'If we had called our bill the "General Holiday Bill" or the "National Holiday Bill" I doubt that it would have been approved. But the more modest name the "Bank Holiday Bill" attracted no attention.'

Thanks to Sir John Lubbock, most of us who work for a living take holiday entitlement for granted.

He changed a problem he couldn't solve into one he could.

THE ONLY WAY IS UP

What was it that sparked the spread of skyscrapers?

Some people say the invention of concrete.

Some people say the invention of steel.

Some people say sheet glass for the windows.

The real answer is none of these.

All these allowed people to build skyscrapers.

But the technology wasn't the issue.

They knew how to build tall buildings centuries before
anyone wanted them.

The real question is what made people want skyscrapers.

The answer is another question: how many flights of stairs
would you be willing to walk up?

One, two, maybe three.

That's it, more than three flights and most people get the
elevator.

And that's the answer.

Without the elevator, people didn't want tall buildings.

People needed an effortless way to get to the top.

So once the elevator was invented people were happy to have
skyscrapers, right?

Well, no, actually.

The 'lifting-platform' was invented hundreds of years before the skyscraper.

But it was only ever used for freight.

Why wasn't it used for people?

Well, mainly because the rope sometimes broke.

When it did, the platform fell and people died.

The real question is: what changed that?

Elisha Otis did.

He'd been a wagon maker and was looking for a safe way to lift goods and people in his factory.

As he'd been a wagon maker he knew about the leaf springs used on carts.

When the wheel goes up the spring bends outwards.

When the wheel goes down the spring bends inwards.

He simply turned the spring upside down, on top of the moving platform so the ends connected to two vertical rails.

When the platform was pulled up, the ends of the spring bent inwards, and the platform was free to move.

If the rope broke, the springs bent outwards and stopped it falling.

Otis tried to sell his invention, but no one was really interested.

He needed a dramatic demonstration, in front of a huge audience.

So, in 1854, he erected it at the New York World's Fair.

In front of everyone, he stood on the platform while it was raised six storeys in the air.

When everyone was watching, his assistant cut the rope with an axe.

The crowd screamed, the platform fell.

But only by a couple of inches.

It stopped as the leaf springs sprang out and gripped the guide rails.

Otis jumped up and down on the platform, but it didn't budge.

In the most dramatic way, he'd made his point.

Now architects could start designing tall buildings.

Otis made skyscrapers desirable because he made them safe.

Today, Otis is the world's largest manufacturer of elevators.

It employs over 60,000 people serving every country on the planet.

They make over $12 billion every year.

Every nine days the equivalent of the entire world's population travels in Otis elevators.

Next time you get in an elevator, look down at the floor.

Odds-on you'll see the word OTIS there.

The name of the man who really understood how to get upstream and change a problem that can't be solved into one that can.

PART EIGHT

BELIEF TRUMPS FACT

BEFORE YOU SELL THE ANSWER, SELL THE NEED

I learned one of the most important lessons about advertising from *Sesame Street*.

Many years ago, I saw an episode in which a young muppet is innocently walking along, singing to himself.

He walks past a suspicious-looking older muppet who has a trench coat with the collar up, dark glasses, and a hat pulled over his eyes.

Older Muppet: Pssst, hey kid, you wanna buy the number 8?

[*He opens his coat and shows the kid a number 8.*]

Younger Muppet: A number 8?

[*The older muppet quickly shuts his coat.*]

OM: Sssssshhhhh!!!!

YM: Why would I want to buy a number 8?

OM: With this number you'd know all sorts of things, kid.

YM: Like what?

OM: Well, suppose you wanted to know what came between seven and nine . . .

[*He opens his jacket and flashes the number.*]

OM: You look at the number.

YM: Gosh.

OM: Yeah, and suppose you wanted to know what 4 plus 4 was . . .

[*He flashes the number again.*]

OM: You check out the number.

YM: That's amazing.

OM: And if you wanted to know what 2 multiplied by 4 was . . .

[*He quickly opens and closes his coat again.*]

OM: You dig the number.

YM: Gosh, I'd like to buy that number 8.

OM: Okay, but come round the corner kid, there's too many people watching here.

The lesson: no one wants anything until they know why they need it.

So before you can sell the answer, you have to sell the need.

Akio Morita, the co-founder of Sony, knew that too.

He got started in electronics at the end of the Second World War.

He bought several dozen wire recorders cheaply from the US military.

But he couldn't sell them because no one saw any need for a recording device.

So Akio Morita wrote a small booklet about all the things you could do with a wire recorder.

Then he distributed these to all the schools in the region.

And all the schools bought all his wire recorders.

Because once they knew what they were for, they wanted one.

Steve Jobs knew that too.

At an Apple conference he went onstage and said, 'I've got three revolutionary products to announce today.

One is an amazing communications device that will change the way we connect with the world.

One is an amazing graphic interface that will change the entire future of gaming.

One is a computer that will change the way we access all knowledge, information and technology.'

When everyone was on the edge of their seats, he took a single object out of his pocket and held it up.

He said, 'The truth is it's one device: the iPhone.'

And, of course, the crowd went wild.

He set up the need, three needs in fact, then provided the answer.

That's what most people don't get.

It's no good providing an answer if you haven't established a need.

NOT ALL SALES ARE GOOD SALES

In 1856, Thomas Burberry founded his company.

In 1879, he invented a fabric called gabardine.

He did this by waterproofing the thread before it was woven.

This meant the fabric could breathe but still remain waterproof.

It was so effective that Roald Amundsen wore it when he became the first man to reach the South Pole in 1911.

Ernest Shackleton wore it for his expedition across the Antarctic in 1914.

In 1924, George Mallory wore it when he became, many people believe, the first man to conquer Everest.

But Thomas Burberry's real claim to fame came in 1914.

He invented the trench coat.

Something to keep British officers warm and dry in the trenches of the First World War.

After the war, his trench coat was so popular that every civilian wanted one.

To make sure everyone knew which was the original, Burberry lined their trench coats with an unusual check pattern.

A sort of brown tartan.

Over the years, the Burberry check became iconic.

So much so, that by the 1970s, people had begun wearing it on the outside of their clothes.

This lining became a coveted design in itself.

No longer anything to do with waterproof garments.

And this is where Burberry made their big mistake.

They assumed that all sales were good sales.

Burberry began selling licences to everyone who wanted one.

The 'Burberry check', and consequently the brand, began appearing everywhere.

Indiscriminately.

From scarves, to shirts, to trousers, to casual jackets, to hats.

So much so that it began to get out of hand.

'Burberry check' began appearing as a joke on inappropriate items of clothing.

On baseball caps, on dog collars, on baby clothes.

And that isn't the image you want for a premium brand.

Pretty soon, the 'Burberry check' became the emblem of the 'chav'.

Which meant no one with any taste or style would be caught dead wearing it.

Burberry had lost its image, its sales, its way.

So, in 2006, Burberry hired a new CEO.

Angela Ahrendts is American.

She flew into London on a cold, grey, damp day to meet the senior executives of Burberry.

Despite the weather, not one of them was wearing any Burberry.

If they didn't want to be seen in their own brand, what chance was there that the public would?

Ahrendts had to set about undoing the damage the previous management had done.

She spent millions of pounds buying back all the licences that had been sold.

Twenty-three different licences, in fact, from companies all over the world.

What seemed like a fast way to make money had all but destroyed the brand.

Before she could get people to reappraise the brand, she had to stop the rot.

And gradually it began to work.

The new designs began to be judged on their own merits.

And they began to sell.

And gradually Burberry turned around.

After she took over, sales more than doubled to £1.9 billion per year and the share price doubled to £13.70.

What Ahrendts knew was that if you have a premium brand, people have to be willing to pay a premium for it.

But they won't do that if everyone in the world has it.

Part of the value of a premium brand is perceived exclusivity.

If everyone has it, it isn't exclusive.

So you can't charge a premium.

Burberry learned the hard way.

Chasing sales isn't always the right thing to do.

ARSE BACKWARDS

During the seventeenth century, a German scientist claimed it was the movement of the trees that created the wind.

This was self-evidently so.

When the trees moved their branches, there was always wind.

When the trees were still, there was no wind.

Just as when someone flaps their arms around, they create a breeze.

But when they are still, there is no breeze.

Wind was the movement of air, so something must be moving it.

Perfect logic.

But being logical doesn't mean it's true.

Because we know it's exactly the other way round.

The German scientist joined up the right dots, but in the wrong order.

Wind moves trees, not vice versa.

But for him the logic was seductive.

His logic was similar to that of most brand advertising.

The logic goes that brand advertising creates reputation.

If we claim our brand is a certain way, then people will see it that way.

If we claim trust, they will trust it.

If we claim reliability, they will believe it's reliable.

If we claim modernity, they'll believe it's modern.

If we claim innovation, they'll believe it's innovative.

They'll join up the dots, but in the wrong order.

Brand is another word for reputation or image.

And you don't get a reputation just by claiming something.

Of course not, first you must *be* something.

Then you get a reputation.

Then you can claim it.

Volkswagen didn't get a reputation for being reliable by running a brand campaign claiming reliability.

Fifty years ago, they ran ads saying, unlike every other car, they were small, inexpensive and sensible.

They had no radiator so the cars didn't freeze in winter.

They were smaller so they got better fuel mileage than other cars.

Their parts were cheaper to replace because they didn't change every year.

That was product advertising, not brand.

But the product advertising built the brand.

Because, over the years, people's experience of VW was that they were solid and dependable.

So, fifty years on, they could run the campaign 'If only everything in life was as reliable as a Volkswagen.'

But they couldn't have run that campaign when they launched, because fifty years earlier they had no reputation for reliability.

The product creates the experience.

The experience creates the reputation.

The reputation creates the brand.

Don't tell me you're a comedian, make me laugh.

IT'S A MATTER OF LIFE AND DEATH

When my son was very small, he asked me about death.

We were driving along on a sunny day.

Suddenly the concept hit him with the weight of a cartoon anvil.

I heard his little voice from the back seat say, 'Daddy, I don't want to die.'

Of course he didn't.

None of us do.

We just get used to the idea over time.

We stop thinking about it.

If the concept of death is difficult for grown-ups, what must it be like for a small child?

You've just discovered what a fantastic and wonderful thing life is.

Then you find out it's all going to be taken away.

You'll lose everything you've got.

Nothing but blackness for eternity.

Unless you're deeply religious, in which case you have stories about various heavens.

How the next life is going to be better than this one.

But I'm not religious, so I couldn't tell my son any of those stories.

I'm not a believer.

I go on evidence, which is what British philosophy was based on: empiricism.

Which means I'm also not an atheist.

Because atheism is the belief that there is definitely no afterlife, that this life is all there is.

I say this is a belief because we can't know it is true.

We don't know there isn't an afterlife any more than we know there is.

But some people seem terrified to accept uncertainty as a position.

Not me.

I'm happy to admit I don't know, until I do.

So I'm agnostic.

Which is another word for keeping an open mind.

Descartes thought doubt was the strongest philosophical tool.

In fact, some philosophers translate 'Cogito, ergo sum' as 'I doubt, therefore I am'.

Certainly scepticism has been the most valuable philosophical tool since Socrates.

Scepticism is what the Enlightenment was based on.

But all this is very difficult to explain to my son in the car.

He's small and confused.

It would be easy to reassure him with fairy tales of paradise.

It would keep him quiet for the time being.

But it would also be an anaesthetic to stop him thinking.

And one day that question will crop up again.

Then he'll find I lied, because I don't believe what I told him.

So that isn't a good solution.

It's a classic advertising problem.

How do you take something very complicated and reduce it to something very simple, while still retaining the core truth?

You always have two ingredients: the product and the audience.

You have to explain the one in terms of the other.

So I said to him, 'You like Sonic the Hedgehog don't you?'

He nodded, he'd play Sonic all day if he could.

I said, 'You know how much fun it is getting through a level on Sonic?'

He nodded again.

I said, 'You know how, when you get to the end of one level, you move up to the next level?'

He smiled, we were in a world he understood now.

'But you don't know what that next level's going to be like until you've finished this level, do you?'

He thought about that.

I said, 'I think that's what death is like. We're having a great time on this level and when we've finished this level, we go on to the next level. But we won't know what the next level is like until we get there.'

And he thought about it and gradually lightened up.

I hadn't lied just to shut him up.

I'd told him the truth in a way that worked for him.

I think that's how it works in advertising or anything else.

TWO WRONGS DON'T MAKE A WRIGHT

A while back, Robin Wight was involved in a project that needed some careful public relations handling.

The most influential man in this area is Alan Parker, founder and chairman of Brunswick PR.

So Robin said to his PA, 'Organize lunch at The Wolseley with Alan Parker for me, would you please?'

Robin's PA called Alan Parker's PA and managed to arrange lunch for the next week, when they were both available.

On the day of the lunch, Robin took all his prepared documents.

He went into the Wolseley and was shown to the table booked in his name.

And there was Alan Parker, already sitting there waiting for him.

But it was the wrong Alan Parker.

It wasn't the PR guru who ran Brunswick PR.

It was Alan Parker the film director.

The man who directed *Bugsy Malone*, *Mississippi Burning*, *Midnight Express* and *Evita*.

This was going to be embarrassing.

What should Robin say?

Obviously, Alan thought Robin had invited him to lunch to discuss shooting some commercials.

Robin realized immediately what had gone wrong.

Robin was founder and chairman of the ad agency WCRS.

In advertising, the most famous Alan Parker was the director.

So, when Robin said Alan Parker, his PA naturally thought he meant this one.

This Alan Parker was the default setting for advertising people.

Unless specified otherwise.

And Robin hadn't specified otherwise, so it wasn't his PA's fault.

Robin thought the best thing to do was carry on with lunch while he worked out what to say.

Strangely enough, Alan Parker didn't seem in a hurry to get down to business either.

The food was good, and they had a very enjoyable lunch.

But eventually Robin thought he'd better confess.

He told Alan the truth, it had been a mix up, he was sorry if he'd wasted his time, sorry but there wasn't a project for him.

Strangely enough, Alan Parker didn't seem disappointed.

In fact, he smiled and said, 'Phew, that's a relief. I was wondering how I was going to let you down. I'm sitting here thinking, how do I tell you I don't do advertising anymore? Especially after you've bought me such a nice lunch.'

Robin said he didn't understand, if Alan didn't do advertising anymore, why did he agree to come and have lunch with him?

Alan Parker said 'When my PA asked if I wanted to have lunch with Robin Wight I thought she said Robin Wright, the Hollywood actress.

I thought she might want to talk to me about a film.'

So Alan Parker thought he was going to lunch with a Hollywood actress.

Robin Wright, who starred in *Forrest Gump* and was married to Sean Penn.

Because Alan's world wasn't advertising any more, it was Hollywood.

And in Hollywood that's the default setting for the name Robin Wight.

Which is why he turned up for the lunch.

And that's a great lesson for all of us.

We think everyone's head is where our head is.

If we think everyone's head is where our head is, we're just talking to ourselves.

WRITING IS EDITING

I once heard a trainee journalist talking about his first day on the job.

He was asked to report on a story.

He investigated it: the facts, the people involved, what happened.

He diligently interviewed everyone and carefully crafted the final piece.

It had an intriguing opening, a coherent middle and a logical end.

When he'd finished, he submitted it to the editor.

Before he'd even got back to his desk the phone was ringing.

It was the editor.

He said 'Rewrite it with all the facts at the front.'

The young journalist said, 'But that would spoil the story.'

The editor said, 'Kid, we put out an entire newspaper every day, top to bottom.

New stories and updates are coming in all the time.

Everything keeps changing until we go to press.

We sometimes have to cut reports, we may have to cut your piece, kid.

When we cut, we cut from the bottom, so make sure all the important stuff, like the facts, are up front.'

So the young journalist had to rewrite his copy.

Because that's the difference between copywriting and a book.

A book may take months to write.

That's okay because people can take weeks to read it, savouring each word.

Copywriting isn't like that.

Copy has to compete for attention.

We can't assume that every word will be pored over, like a book.

That's what made Ernest Hemingway different as a writer.

Hemingway trained as a journalist.

Before he became a novelist, he worked on the *Kansas City Star*.

He learned the paper's style, it became his guide to writing: 'Use short sentences. Use short paragraphs. Use vigorous English.'

He learned to get the most from the least, to prune language.

Later in life Hemingway would call this style 'The Iceberg Theory'.

By stating the bare minimum, you let the reader's imagination add the part unsaid, the part below the surface.

In writing classes at universities it's now known as 'The Theory of Omission.'

In 1928, the *New York Times* wrote of Hemingway's first novel: 'No amount of analysis can convey the quality of *The Sun Also Rises*. It is a truly gripping story, told in lean, hard, athletic, narrative prose that puts more "literary" English to shame.'

Hemingway's style influenced an entire generation of writers.

In 1952 he won the Pulitzer Prize.

In 1954 he won the Nobel Prize.

The *Transatlantic Review* said Hemingway 'actively trimmed the verbal "fat" off his own style, and flexed his writer's muscles in assaulting conventional taste.'

Hemingway put it differently. He said, 'Writing is architecture, not interior decoration.'

IT'S GOOD TO TALK

People don't like thinking about death.

And they certainly don't like talking about it.

My mum's generation didn't mind talking about it.

When I was in my twenties, my dad got cancer.

It was terminal and he was in hospital.

I'd never had anyone really close to me die before so I didn't know how his death would affect me.

I thought I'd better take care of the arrangements while he was alive, in case I wasn't able to afterwards.

I told Mum I was going to get Dad a grave in the local cemetery.

Mum said she'd like a double grave so that, later on, she could be buried with Dad.

My aunt Polly was at Mum's at the time, having a cup of tea.

Auntie Polly was Mum's sister and she'd married Dad's brother, Uncle Fred, so the families were close.

Auntie Polly asked me if I could get a grave for her and Uncle Fred next to Mum and Dad.

So they'd all be together.

I said I'd see if I could.

Then they both said, 'What about Uncle Harry?'

Uncle Harry was their younger brother who lived nearby.

He never married and, being older sisters, they felt very protective.

They didn't want him left out.

They asked me if I could get a grave for Uncle Harry next to them.

So I went to the cemetery and asked if I could choose three plots: a single and two doubles.

I didn't like the newer part of the cemetery, it was near the bypass and a bit noisy.

But there were three plots together in the older, quieter part of the cemetery.

So I put a deposit on those.

Then I brought Mum and Auntie Polly over to see what they thought of them.

I said, 'Look, Mum, you and Dad will be just here, Auntie Polly and Uncle Fred will be next door, then Uncle Harry will be on the end.

There's a nice tree here so there's lots of shade, and there's a bench under it, so you can come and visit Dad. What do you think?'

Auntie Polly and Mum both said they liked their spots.

Mum pointed to a small brick building nearby and said, 'I tell you what I like best, the toilets are just there.'

That stopped me.

I laughed and I said, 'Don't worry about that, Mum, you won't be getting up to use the toilet.'

Mum frowned. She said, 'I'm not thinking about me, I'm thinking about the people coming to visit me.

If they get caught short at least they'll have somewhere to go.'

Now that's a mum's mum.

Even after she's dead, she's worried about visitors needing the loo.

But what I liked best was the matter-of-fact way we talked about it.

Nowadays, of course, if anything is controversial we don't talk about it.

We sweep it under the carpet.

Just in case, God forbid, it should make us uncomfortable.

So we avoid talking about things.

And that can't be good.

Stopping talking about things is the first stage in stopping thinking about things.

WHERE ISN'T EVERYONE LOOKING?

(Warning: this piece contains lots of Daves.)

Dave Dye was telling me about Dave Wakefield.

Dave Dye says Dave Wakefield is the best typographer there is.

But what fascinated him wasn't his understanding of type design.

Dave Dye said Dave Wakefield told him he'd been in a band when he was young.

Okay, nothing surprising there, lots of people were in bands when they were young.

But Dave Wakefield says he was in a band with David Bowie (or David Jones, as he was then).

This fascinated Dave Dye.

He asked Dave Wakefield what David Bowie was like as a youngster.

Dave Wakefield said they always knew he was going to be a star.

Just because he wasn't anything like the rest of them.

Dave Wakefield said it was his music.

The rest of them just collected their favourite type of records: mainly rock and roll.

But David Bowie collected everything, really weird stuff they'd never heard of.

Stuff they wouldn't dream of listening to.

Show tunes from Broadway musicals, oompah music from brass bands, country and western music, Japanese music, whale songs, men playing the spoons, opera.

Dave Wakefield said the rest of the group didn't even know a lot of this music existed, much less where to buy it.

And it certainly wasn't the sort of thing they wanted to listen to.

But you could tell David Bowie was taking it all in.

And he was going to use it one day.

And Dave Wakefield said you could feel that unusual star quality.

Nobody else around was listening to anything like it.

So there wouldn't be anyone around like him.

Not wanting to look where everyone else was looking.

Because that was the stuff that had all been done before.

Knowing the real opportunity was where everyone else wasn't looking.

There was an entire world of music out there just waiting.

And no one else was even looking at it.

He could have it all to himself.

And the different combinations he could make would be

fresh and unusual because his influences were like no one
else's.

I loved it when Dave Dye told me that.

Because it was exactly what I'd heard, and watched,
advertising greats John Webster, Paul Arden and Ron Collins
doing.

Looking where no one else was looking.

Paul Arden looked in art galleries for unusual modern art.

John Webster looked in American comics and British
propaganda from the 1940s and 1950s.

Ron Collins looked at Renaissance art, Botticelli in particular.

Like David Bowie, these guys started out with a huge
advantage.

Everyone else was fishing in the same little advertising pond.

These guys were fishing in a huge ocean of 2,000 years of
creativity.

And that's what star quality probably is.

It's about confidence.

If you don't have the confidence to be different, to stand out,
you'll want to be part of the herd.

The reassurance of looking in the same places as everyone else.

But then, of course, your work will end up looking like
everyone else's.

PART NINE

CREATIVITY IS MESSY

LIFE'S A PITCH

Paul Smith was a producer, he made programmes for television.

At least he did when he could sell them.

He'd been trying to sell one particular idea for two years.

It was a quiz show where the contestant had to guess the correct answer from a choice of four shown on screen.

If the contestant got all the answers right, eventually they could win a million pounds.

Smith had sent his idea to the BBC, Channel 4, Channel 5, but no one would touch it.

What kept him going was the fact that one person loved it: Claudia Rosencrantz at ITV.

She showed it to her boss, David Liddiment.

But Liddiment was worried about the whole idea.

He told her he could lose a million pounds an episode with the answers on the screen.

Paul Smith said he wanted a chance to present the show to Liddiment himself.

Smith knew there was no point in an argument.

The only way was to get him to play the game.

So as soon as he met Liddiment he asked him to take his wallet out.

Then he asked him how much was in it. Liddiment counted out £210.

Smith said, 'Okay add an IOU for £40, making it £250, and put it all on the desk.'

Then Smith took out an envelope containing £250 and placed it next to Liddiment's money.

He said, 'If you can answer a question, the whole £500 is yours. If not, you lose your £250.'

He asked him the question and he showed him the choice of answers.

Liddiment started asking Claudia Rosencrantz which she would pick.

Smith said, 'Now you're using your "phone-a-friend" lifeline.'

Liddiment said okay, but he and Claudia couldn't agree on the answer.

Smith said, 'You could use your "50:50" lifeline.'

Liddiment said okay, so Smith took away two of the answers. And Liddiment guessed the right one.

Smith gave him the whole £500 and said, 'That's all yours, unless you want to double it by answering the next question.'

And he put an envelope containing £500 down next to it.

Smith asked Liddiment the next question.

Then he showed him the four choices.

Liddiment started discussing them with Claudia Rosencrantz.

Smith said, 'Hang on, you've already used the "phone-a-friend" lifeline. You can't use it again.'

Liddiment asked what options he had left.

Smith said, 'You can use your "ask-the-audience" lifeline.'

So Liddiment opened his office door and discussed it with the staff sitting outside.

But everyone had a different opinion on the answer.

Liddiment frowned and closed the door.

He said to Smith, 'No, I'm going to take the £500 instead.'

And at that point, Paul Smith knew he'd sold the idea.

Because Liddiment saw he wouldn't lose a million pounds an episode.

He had experienced loss-aversion.

As Nobel Prize-winning psychologist Daniel Kahneman has shown, fear of losing is more powerful than the prospect of gains.

And so David Liddiment was hooked.

In fact, he loved the idea so much he arranged to run the show every single night of the week.

And *Who Wants To Be A Millionaire?* went on to pull in bigger audiences than *EastEnders*.

And it only happened because Paul Smith stopped expecting his client to understand his idea rationally, and got his client to feel it.

Because that's where the sell happens.

Paul Smith moved the sell from what Kahneman calls System Two thinking (the slow, rational mind) to System One thinking (the fast, emotional mind).

As in any sell, desire must precede permission.

ONE WAY TO CHANGE THE GAME

In 1945, Sam Shoen was discharged from the US Navy.

He and his wife wanted to move from Los Angeles to

Portland, Oregon.

The two cities are about a thousand miles apart.

They had a lot of stuff they wanted to take with them.

But hiring a firm of professional movers was something the

young married couple couldn't afford.

So they checked out the cost of hiring a trailer.

They found you could hire trailers in LA at a daily rate.

The downside was, of course, that when you'd finished you

had to return it.

This was fine for people who lived in LA.

You rent it, you use it, you take it back.

But it wouldn't work for Sam and his wife.

They would have to drive 1,000 miles to Oregon.

Then bring the trailer 1,000 miles back to LA.

Then drive 1,000 miles back to Oregon again.

That didn't make any sense.

So they had to leave most of their possessions behind in LA,

and just take what they could squeeze into their car.

On the drive to Oregon, Sam kept grumbling about it.

Millions of young men all over America were being

discharged from the military.

They'd be moving around the country to different jobs.

They'd all be in the same situation as Sam and his wife.

They'd all need to rent a trailer, but just to go one-way.

And there was no company where they could rent one to do that.

As they drove they talked more.

Sam thought it was a game-changing idea to start a one-way trailer rental company.

His wife said, 'How could the company get it back if they dropped it off hundreds of miles away?'

Sam said that with all those people moving around the country someone was sure to be coming back the other way and needing a trailer.

If you had enough trailers you could just leave them all over the country.

Sam's wife said, 'But where could you leave them?'

Sam thought for a minute.

Then he said, 'How about petrol stations?'

To rent a trailer you need a car, and cars need petrol, so that's a perfect fit.

They could split the fees with the owners, and most petrol stations are out of town so space won't be problem.

And if the trailers had the name painted on the side they would sit around like posters advertising themselves.

And people would see the name wherever the trailer went and know you could rent them.

And so they started to see if they could think of a name.

And by the end of the journey they had a great name.

U-Haul.

A name that says exactly what the product does, in a catchy way.

A name that's also a call-to-action.

A name that's a mnemonic so it can't be copied.

By the end of 1945, U-Haul had thirty trailers in locations across the northwest USA.

But by 1955, U-Haul had 10,000 trailers all across America.

And by 1959, U-Haul had 42,000 trailers.

Everyone thinks car-rental companies invented one-way rental, but they didn't.

It wasn't until 1954, nearly ten years later, that National Car Rental became the first to copy it.

Soon Hertz, Avis, Budget, Dollar and Alamo all followed suit.

Now it's accepted practice.

Pick a car up in one city, leave it in another.

Sam started his company with $5,000 dollars in 1945.

Now U-Haul is a multi-billion dollar business with 16,000 dealerships across the USA and Canada.

So was one-way trailer rental a game-changing idea?

Let's look at the numbers.

In North America today, 50 million people move every year.

The average person moves eleven times in their lifetime.

75% of all those moves are done using trailers.

Every day, U-Haul vehicles cover enough mileage to go
around the world 194 times.

Or, to the moon and back 20 times.

Every day.

I think we can call that a game-changing idea.

KEEP IT DARK

When Ridley Scott finally got the financing to make *Blade Runner* it wasn't as much as he wanted.

The Hollywood studio didn't believe in it as much as he did.

So they cut costs.

Ridley wanted to build a futuristic Los Angeles set for the movie.

But all the studio would give him was an existing back lot.

Part of a generic 1920s town they had built ages ago.

An unused set where they used to shoot gangster movies.

All set in prohibition times.

Because gangster movies had fallen out of fashion the buildings and streets on set were decayed and peeling.

Ridley looked at it and wondered what to do.

Obviously he felt insulted, the studio clearly didn't take his film seriously.

What were his options?

He could tell the studio to shove it.

But if he did that it would almost certainly be the end of the movie.

And probably the end of his film career in Hollywood too.

So what could he do?

How could he shoot a futuristic science-fiction film about

mutant robots in a set designed for black and white films about gangsters?

Ridley thought it over.

And he thought, the future is never going to be simply about the future.

The future isn't just brand new buildings, and brand new cars, and brand new everything.

The future is always about the latest things, overlaid on what came before.

He thought, I could overlay the future onto this set from the past.

And he added shiny aluminium piping to the outside of the buildings.

And he added neon signs to the outside of the buildings.

And people in futuristic, plastic clothes carrying neon umbrellas.

And travelling airships with massive outdoor TV screens.

And all these futuristic props overlaid on the grungy old buildings just emphasized how the future always elbows the past aside.

But it did something much more important.

Because of all the neon, Ridley decided to shoot the movie at night.

The neon would show up better in the dark.

But it would also throw all the buildings into the background.

To increase the effect he'd shoot in the rain.

Giving the movie the feel of a deserted and bypassed planet earth.

Perfect for a story about returning mutant robots looking for their history.

And the set did something even more important than that.

The cumulative effect was to give the entire movie an all-pervading dark, ominous, threatening, sinister mood.

It launched an entirely new genre of filmmaking.

Noir science fiction.

Blade Runner became the movie that Ridley Scott says he is most proud of.

Since its release, it has won nearly forty awards worldwide.

It has been reissued in seven different versions.

It is considered a masterpiece.

After *Blade Runner*, Ridley Scott's Hollywood career took off.

He went on to make many massively successful movies.

He has subsequently been knighted.

And in a recent Hollywood poll, was voted one of the most important directors in the world.

All by taking a problem and turning it into an opportunity.

CREATIVITY IS MESSY

João Magueijo is a physics professor at Imperial College, London.

He is Portuguese and has lived in England for twenty-five years.

He's written a book about us.

He says the English are 'one of the most rigid and rotten societies in Europe, possibly the world'.

He says, 'I never met such a group of animals, English culture is pathologically violent.'

He says, 'Oral sex is not considered a sexual act among the English.

It is something a woman can perform on a stranger whose name she doesn't even know, no one cares.'

He says, 'When you visit English homes, they are all so disgusting that even my grandmother's poultry cage is cleaner.'

He says, 'It is not unusual to drink 12 pints, or 2 huge buckets of beer, per person. Even a horse would get drunk with this but in England it is standard practice. In England, real men have to drink like sponges and throw up everything at the end of the evening.'

He says, 'They say "it's grim up north" and now I see why:

people in the north are incredibly obese, men and women with three-metre waists made of fat and lard. Blackpool beach is an ideal place to see these "human whales".'

This book was on the bestseller list in Portugal for six months.

So, given the professor is so disgusted with us, why did he stay in England for so long?

He says, 'I love the British sense of humour. I love the tolerance, the creativity and the madness of the people. There is an incapacity for institutional repression, which I like.'

I think that's really interesting.

What he calls the 'incapacity for institutional repression'.

In other words: rebelliousness, questioning the rules, a refusal to bow to authority.

The problem is that you can't have it both ways.

You can't have an exciting, dynamic, creative society and one which also follows all the rules of decorum and good taste.

You can't follow the rules while you're breaking the rules.

That is the dichotomy.

It reminds me of a conversation I heard at dinner one evening between Bob Brooks and Oscar Grillo.

Bob was a brilliant film director from New York.

Oscar is a brilliant animator from Buenos Aires.

Both loved London, but Bob was grumbling about it.

Bob said, 'The problem is nothing fucking works: the

goddamn buses, the goddamn trains, the goddamn roads. Nothing fucking works'.

Oscar said, 'Of course it doesn't work. Why do you think we come here? What do you think we want: fucking Switzerland?'

And that summed it up for me.

England, especially London, is messy and that's what makes it interesting.

Nelson's Column in Trafalgar Square celebrates one of our greatest naval victories.

Look up the crew list on Nelson's flagship, HMS *Victory*.

They were English, Scottish, Welsh and Irish.

But they were also: Danish, Norwegian, Canadian, German, Dutch, Swedish, Swiss, Maltese, Portuguese, Brazilian, Indian, Jamaican, African, American, even French.

And that was just one ship.

What I've always loved about London is that, like New York, it attracts creativity (and that means rebels) from all over the world.

The best thrives because it's the best.

Not because it's the nicest.

But, of course, that can get messy, that's the price you pay.

Orson Welles summed it up best in *The Third Man*.

'In Italy, for thirty years under the Borgias, they had warfare, terror, murder and bloodshed, but they produced Michelangelo, Leonardo da Vinci and the Renaissance. In Switzerland they had brotherly love, 500 years of democracy and peace, and what did that produce? The cuckoo clock.'

I also like what Voltaire said about the English.
'The English are like their own beer: the dregs are at the bottom, the top is nothing but froth, but the middle is quite excellent.'

HOW 'LEARNINGS' PREVENT THINKING

There was a terrific article in the *New Yorker*.

It was called 'Money Talks' by John Lanchester.

It's about the way learning a terminology destroys thinking.

He describes how, in order to make certain financial practices more respectable, they are first described in metaphors.

Then the metaphor becomes terminology.

Then the terminology becomes fact.

Which means no one ever questions it.

'Hedge fund' is a good example.

In the early days, it simply meant betting both ways.

So you wouldn't lose everything on a single bet.

You'd effectively put a 'hedge' or barrier around your investment.

You'd hedge your bets.

Hedge funds sprang up, firms that were specialists in spreading your investments so you couldn't lose.

But competition between them became fierce.

And financial return became more important than safety.

And hedge funds became places for increasingly exotic, and risky, investments.

In 2010, there were 7,200 hedge funds; 750 went bust.

In 2011, another 873 went bust, in 2012, another 904.

What went wrong was that no one questioned the term 'hedge fund'.

Where was the hedge, the barrier, protecting the investment?

Another example Lanchester gives is the term 'securities'.

Security originally meant making something safe.

But in finance, 'security' now means converting something into a tradeable asset.

And that tradeable asset can be anything.

From future royalties on David Bowie's albums to flaky mortgages on low-income houses.

Which is exactly what led to the worldwide financial crash of 2008.

So, not very secure after all.

But no one questioned the word 'security'.

They learned the terminology, and just accepted it as fact.

He gives other examples of terms that no one questions:

'Credit' now means debt.

'Inflation' actually means money is worth less.

'Leverage' strangely means borrowing money.

'Synergy' in fact means sacking people.

'Bail out' oddly means pouring money in.

And what was originally a series of metaphors to describe a process has become a terminology, then a fact.

And young people learning the trade believe they are learning facts.

Which is exactly the same as advertising.

To make it respectable, everything has been turned into terminology.

Which is impenetrable, so it can't be questioned.

It can't be questioned so it must be fact.

Listen to any meeting:

Brand audit, cluster groups, segmentation, penetration, CRM, SEO, CSR, ROI, KPI, UGC, integrated, transactional, native advertising, value-added, differentials, core competency, ideation, hygiene factors, demographics, psychographics, profile testing, deliverables, storytelling, narrowcasting, acquisition, content, data capture, rate card, deep dive.

How often do we question any of that terminology?

But if we don't question it, we can't understand it.

We're just learning it parrot fashion.

And we lose focus on the purpose of what we're supposed to be doing.

WORKING WHILE YOU'RE ASLEEP

When Michael Caine was just becoming famous, so were his
mates.

Other young actors and people he knew.

Nowadays it sounds like name-dropping because they're all
famous.

But at the time, they were all just mates: Terence Stamp,
David Hemmings, Albert Finney, Tom Courtenay, Sean
Connery, Peter O'Toole.

They'd work, and party, and get drunk together, and give each
other advice on their careers.

Just the way everyone else does.

One of this group was a hairdresser.

He'd opened a shop in the West End and he was doing okay.

In fact, better than okay, he was really fashionable.

He was a cockney called Vidal Sassoon.

He had a different style of cutting hair that didn't depend on
the artificial 1950s look.

Until Sassoon, most hairdressers would cut the hair then
spray it into position with tons of hairspray.

Vidal Sassoon did it the other way round.

First he washed and dried the hair and let it hang naturally.

Then he cut it into shape.

So it always fell the way it was cut.

This wasn't just a totally new way to cut hair, it was a totally new look.

All the *Vogue* models wanted Sassoon to personally cut their hair, people like Jean Shrimpton and Twiggy.

Even top designers like Mary Quant and film stars like Mia Farrow.

So Sassoon's Mayfair salon was doing very well, but despite that Michael Caine felt like giving him some advice.

It was in the early hours of the morning, after an evening's partying, over a bottle of wine.

We've all been there.

Michael Caine said, 'Look Vidal, you're doing alright, you're making a few bob, but you're not going to get *really* rich the way you're going.'

Sassoon asked him what he meant.

Michael Caine said, 'It's like my old dad said, the really rich have got something going that makes them money while they're asleep.

Look at it this way, you're cutting hair and you're doing alright, but everyone wants you personally to cut their hair, and you're only one bloke.

There's a limit to how many haircuts you can do in a day: six, seven, eight.

You want to set something up that doesn't depend on you personally cutting hair.

I'm in film: the money keeps rolling in even after I've finished acting in that film.

Same with pop stars, the money from the records keeps coming in, even after they've finished singing.

Find a way to get something going in this hairdresser game that keeps working for you even when you're asleep.'

Vidal Sassoon went quiet.

This was good advice.

He'd never thought of that.

Expand his business beyond the physical limits of what he could actually do himself.

Michael Caine went to bed, but Vidal Sassoon kept thinking.

Within a year, he opened the Sassoon Academy in Mayfair, teaching young professionals how to cut and care for hair.

This established him as thought leader in the field of beautiful hair.

Then he opened Sassoon Academies all across the USA, Canada and Australia.

He became the most celebrated hairdresser in the world.

Meanwhile he launched a hair-care range featuring dozens of different products.

The range with his name on it became massive.

Sassoon was teaching people around the world to cut hair his way.

All these hairdressers would become evangelists, who would only recommend Sassoon haircare products.

In 1982, sales were $110 million worldwide, the equivalent of half a billion dollars today.

Just by listening to Michael Caine's old dad's simple cockney logic.

'Get something going for you that works while you're asleep.'

THE END OF THE WORLD

In 1914, Kit Wykeham-Musgrave was 15 years old.

He was a midshipman serving on the cruiser HMS *Aboukir*.

Suddenly, there was a huge explosion.

The massive warship began to list, it started sinking.

Sirens were sounding, men were yelling, everyone was running.

His first thought was to get away from the ship before it went down.

He jumped into the ice-cold water.

He started to swim for his life.

He knew that when a big ship went down, the suction pulled anyone near it under.

But he was young and determined to survive.

He swam around until another cruiser stopped to pick up survivors.

Kit was one of the lucky ones.

He clambered aboard HMS *Hogue* and stood dripping wet on the deck.

When another massive explosion rocked that ship.

HMS *Hogue* went down a lot faster than HMS *Aboukir*.

Many men, who couldn't get out in time, drowned trapped below deck.

Again Kit jumped overboard just before the ship sank, and again he swam.

He'd been on two ships that sank within minutes of each other.

An unbelievable experience.

He'd survived once, could he survive again?

Luckily he was young and fit, his desire to live gave him energy.

Kit swam until he was picked up by a third cruiser.

On board HMS *Cressy*, he was wrapped in a blanket and given a mug of hot cocoa.

He knew he was one very lucky boy.

Then a massive explosion rocked HMS *Cressy*, and she started to sink.

Men jumped overboard, men were trapped below deck.

He was back in the water trying to escape the suction as the ship went down.

Kit had been sunk three times in less than an hour.

Now he had no energy, all he could do was cling on to some driftwood.

There were no other ships around to swim to anyway.

A squadron of three cruisers had just been sent to the bottom by the one thing no one at the Admiralty took seriously.

A submarine.

Submarines were new, nobody could see what use they were.

They were fragile, slow, they only had one small gun.

All the admirals knew the war would be won by big ships with big guns.

Ships like the three cruisers that had just been sunk.

By a submarine.

At the start of the war, Germany only had a few U-boats.

They didn't think they'd bother building any more.

None of the admirals on either side could see much point.

Until the U9 sank HMS *Aboukir*, HMS *Hogue*, and HMS *Cressy*, and 1,397 sailors died.

In an hour, all conventional views on naval warfare were obsolete.

What had seemed tiny and vulnerable was suddenly deadly.

And the old world ended and the new world began.

Germany immediately began developing a powerful submarine fleet.

In fact, in two world wars, Germany's U-boats were the things that came closest to winning them the war.

The weapon that all the admirals had said was just a useless toy.

Kit Wykeham-Musgrave was eventually picked up by a Dutch trawler.

He, and every other sailor, learned a very valuable lesson about submarines and experts.

They don't know what they don't know, until they find out they don't know it.

Acknowledgements

I'd like to thank my literary agent Jonathan Conway and especially Jon Butler, who had faith in some rough sheets of A4 and helped nurse them all the way into a proper book.

I'd especially like to thank Zennor Compton, who painstakingly went over every single word with a magnifying glass.

Anywhere it's properly written it's down to Zennor and anywhere it isn't it's down to me.

extracts reading groups
competitions books new
discounts extracts
extracts discounts
competitions
books new
reading groups extracts
events books
extracts books
books new reading groups
interviews
events extracts
discounts
new books events
events new
discounts extracts discounts

www.panmacmillan.com

extracts events reading groups
competitions books extracts new